BFI Film Classics

The BFI Film Classics series introduces, interprets and celebrates landmarks of world cinema. Each volume offers an argument for the film's 'classic' status, together with discussion of its production and reception history, its place within a genre or national cinema, an account of its technical and aesthetic importance, and in many cases, the author's personal response to the film.

For a full list of titles in the series, please visit
https://www.bloomsbury.com/uk/series/bfi-film-classics/

Billy Elliot

James Leggott

THE BRITISH FILM INSTITUTE
Bloomsbury Publishing Plc, 50 Bedford Square, London, WC1B 3DP, UK
Bloomsbury Publishing Inc, 1385 Broadway, New York, NY 10018, USA
Bloomsbury Publishing Ireland, 29 Earlsfort Terrace, Dublin 2, D02 AY28, Ireland

BLOOMSBURY is a trademark of Bloomsbury Publishing Plc

First published in Great Britain 2025 by Bloomsbury on behalf of the
British Film Institute, 21 Stephen Street, London, W1T 1LN
www.bfi.org.uk

The BFI is a cultural charity, a National Lottery distributor, and the UK's lead organisation for film and the moving image. We believe society needs stories. Film, television and the moving image bring them to life, helping us to connect and understand each other better. We share the stories of yesterday, search for the stories of today, and shape the stories of tomorrow.

Copyright © James Leggott 2025

James Leggott has asserted his right under the Copyright, Designs and Patents Act, 1988, to be identified as author of this work.

For legal purposes the Acknowledgments on p. 6 constitute an extension of this copyright page.

Cover artwork: © Klara Gryglicka
Series cover design: Louise Dugdale
Series text design: Ketchup/SE14
Images from *Billy Elliot* (Stephen Daldry, 2000), © Tiger Aspect; *My Ain Folk* (Bill Douglas, 1973), British Film Institute Production Board; *Kes* (Ken Loach, 1969), © Woodfall Films Ltd; *The Old Oak* (Ken Loach, 2023), © Sixteen Oak Ltd/Why Not Productions/BBC/Wild Bunch/France 2 Cinéma/Les Films du Fleuve/BFI
Film stills courtesy BFI National Archive

All rights reserved. No part of this publication may be: i) reproduced or transmitted in any form, electronic or mechanical, including photocopying, recording or by means of any information storage or retrieval system without prior permission in writing from the publishers; or ii) used or reproduced in any way for the training, development or operation of artificial intelligence (AI) technologies, including generative AI technologies. The rights holders expressly reserve this publication from the text and data mining exception as per Article 4(3) of the Digital Single Market Directive (EU) 2019/790.

Bloomsbury Publishing Plc does not have any control over, or responsibility for, any third-party websites referred to or in this book. All internet addresses given in this book were correct at the time of going to press. The author and publisher regret any inconvenience caused if addresses have changed or sites have ceased to exist, but can accept no responsibility for any such changes.

A catalogue record for this book is available from the British Library.

A catalog record for this book is available from the Library of Congress.

ISBN: PB: 978-1-8390-2780-2
       ePDF: 978-1-8390-2782-6
       ePUB: 978-1-8390-2781-9

Printed and bound in India

For product safety related questions contact productsafety@bloomsbury.com.

To find out more about our authors and books visit www.bloomsbury.com and sign up for our newsletters.

Contents

Acknowledgments	6
Introduction	7
1 Raising *Billy Elliot*	13
2 Dancer: *Billy Elliot* by Numbers	37
3 Go, Billy! The Legacy of *Billy Elliot*	77
Notes	90
Credits	99

Acknowledgments

I'm grateful to Roanna Benn, Greg Brenman, Peter Darling, Jon Finn, Lee Hall and Stephen Warbeck for sharing their reflections on *Billy Elliot* with me, and to Lee Hall for letting me see the first draft of the script. Along the way, I've been generously assisted by David Forrest, Hugo Glover, the staff of the BFI Reuben Library, the anonymous reviewers of the manuscript and the commissioning, editorial, production and design staff at Bloomsbury, including Rebecca Barden, Anna Coatman, Barbara Cohen Bastos and Sophie Contento.

This is dedicated to my family.

Introduction

There are so many Billy Elliots pirouetting across the stage, you can barely count them.

It's the curtain call of a special performance of *Billy Elliot: The Musical* at the Victoria Palace Theatre in London, also being beamed live to cinemas around the world. First staged in 2005, the musical was developed by some of the creative team that had collaborated on the original *Billy Elliot* film of 2000, about a young boy from a coal-mining town in North East England overcoming family prejudice and financial hardship to realise his dream of being a ballet dancer. In the extended finale of the celebratory performance on 28 September 2014, a full troupe of young actors – all of whom have played the main character on stage before – deliver a joyfully energetic routine, catapulting on and off stage in dizzying permutations.

One of the performers is an eighteen-year-old Tom Holland, who would in time become as famous as the original *Billy Elliot* boy, Jamie Bell. But he's just one of thirty graceful embodiments of the so-called 'Billy Elliot effect'. The term has been used to connote, variously, the increased popularity of dance training among boys, creative achievements that challenge expectations of class and gender, and – with regards to the British film industry specifically – the fairy-tale phenomenon of a low-budget movie generating critical acclaim, international success and a global, cross-media franchise of stagings and spin-offs.

If *Billy Elliot* has a reputation as both a narrative and agent of transformation, it also had a significant impact on the careers of those responsible for its development. It was a first taste of feature production for writer Lee Hall and director Stephen Daldry. The convoluted production credit at the head of film – 'Working Title Films and BBC Films in association with the Arts Council of England

8 | BFI FILM CLASSICS

present a Tiger Aspect Pictures Production in association with WT²' – betrays a complex origin story that demands unpicking, but its success brought prestige to all parties involved, in addition to overnight fame for the teenage Jamie Bell.

Since its UK theatrical release in September 2000, *Billy Elliot* has provided rich pickings for critics contemplating its place within the British social-realist tradition and its reconstruction of an industrial dispute widely regarded as a defining moment in British political, economic and cultural history. The UK miners' strike (1984–5), led by Arthur Scargill's National Union of Mineworkers (NUM) against the National Coal Board (NCB), was a divisive and ultimately unsuccessful response to the Conservative government's plan to close collieries deemed to be uneconomical. The bitter defeat of the trade union was a victory for Prime Minister Margaret Thatcher, but the longer-term impact was the privatisation and decline of the coal industry, and – for mining communities like those depicted in *Billy Elliot* – the devastating personal and social effects of widespread and continuing unemployment. In the ensuing flood

Arthur Scargill with NUM supporter wearing Thatcher mask, Stoke, 1984 (*Manchester Daily Express*/SSPL/Getty Images)

of academic responses, the film's allusions, representational politics, narrative schemes and industrial strategies were exhaustively mined for meaning. Among scholars of British media culture, certain critical positions became dominant. In an early response, John Hill identified Billy as a Blairite emblem of post-industrial regeneration,[1] and many commentators yoked the film with *Brassed Off* (1996) and *The Full Monty* (1997) to define a cycle of realist comedies about northern, working-class males performing their way out of obsolescence. For Paul Marris, such films would effectively 'cast the crisis of post-industrialism as the crisis of masculinity'.[2] At the industrial level, the participation of WT^2 – a short-lived, low-budget offshoot of Working Title – encouraged readings within the context of the parent company's mid- or transatlantic strategies of production. For some, the film was illustrative of British cinema's subordinate, neocolonial position in relation to Hollywood.[3]

But there were aspects of the *Billy Elliot* phenomenon that received limited attention, such as how the film's tone and attitude were shaped by creative personnel with a mostly theatrical background (the case for its author, director, choreographer and composer), or how its East Durham setting situated it within a particular tradition of representation and artistry. Many commentators noted the film's explicit conceptual and narrative debt to Ken Loach's *Kes* (1969), but the influence of British film directors Bill Douglas and Terence Davies, and of parallel developments in 1990s dance and physical theatre, were not so well observed.

The subsequent *Billy Elliot* musical gave Lee Hall, Stephen Daldry, producer Jon Finn and choreographer Peter Darling opportunity to revisit and augment their film work, now with musical input by Elton John. In interviews, they have conveyed that they consider the stage *Billy Elliot* to be the definitive version of the material,[4] in the way that it allows for more assertive political commentary, and a more nuanced representation of Billy's home community. Could this be one of the reasons why the original film today seems somewhat eclipsed by its own influence? The historian

Dominic Sandbrook has described the *Billy Elliot* phenomenon as one of the outstanding cultural accomplishments of recent years, the 'perfect advertisement for the extraordinary global appeal of the British imagination'.[5] But as film scholar Neil Archer has observed, there is a 'palimpsestic' aspect – that is, a dense process of layering – to any triumphant narrative that culminates in a 'West End show about a boy who, in the end, makes it in a West End show'.[6] The *Billy Elliot* story itself began with a leap of imagination, not in the former coalfields of Durham, North East England, but the university town of Durham, North Carolina, where the young Geordie writer Lee Hall had an idea about a boy in a tutu.

1 Raising *Billy Elliot*

The critical and commercial triumph of *Billy Elliot* led to the film, its leading character and its production team being widely hailed as a success story for the UK's creative sector. The storyline about a community coming together to finance Billy's travel to a London audition has a correlation with the multipart funding and mentorship of the film from origin to release. And its allusions to an array of musicians, films and performers – whether through direct citation or mere suggestion – communicate the broad scope of cultural forces that shaped its evolution and production, from British and Hollywood film-making to experimental dance and regional theatrical traditions. However, the writer Lee Hall is the rational origin point, given his explanation of the story as a form of fantasy autobiography, drawing upon his own background and creative career.

Perhaps unexpectedly, the idea for the film took flight following Hall's move from the UK to the US in the early 1990s. Born in Newcastle upon Tyne in 1966, and from a working-class background, Hall had only recently decided on a professional writing career, having followed his time as a student of English Literature and Drama at Cambridge University with several administrative roles in the theatre world. But he had already made some useful connections, not least with the theatre director Stephen Daldry. Their paths had first crossed in the mid-1980s, when

Lee Hall (courtesy Lee Hall)

the teenage Hall – fully immersed in Tyneside's vibrant youth theatre scene – wrote a play for his school, which was later performed at the Crucible Theatre, Sheffield, where Daldry was working as an assistant director. About five years later, when Hall was employed at the Gate Theatre in Notting Hill, he happened to bump into Daldry again, who asked him to be involved on the administrative side of a stage project. Through this association, Hall was introduced to Kate Rowland, a producer at BBC Radio Drama, who commissioned his first piece of professional writing, *I Luv U Jimmy Spud* (1995), about a young Geordie boy with a dying father.[7]

Billy Elliot was Hall's first film project to reach fruition, but his first screenplay experience had been the commissioning of a feature version of his *Jimmy Spud* radio script. At this point, around 1995, he was living in New York City, having gone to stay with Daldry. Not only had he never thought about being a screenwriter, but he had also never read a film script and moreover had 'hardly ever been to the cinema'.[8] Following a crash course of video rentals and screenwriting guides, he considered his first screenplay to be a creative breakthrough but distanced himself from its eventual emergence as *Gabriel & Me* (2001), which he considered a 'botched job ruined by its total lack of humour'.[9] However, his original screenplay was used as a sample script to solicit future commissions, the first to bear fruit being *Billy Elliot*.

While hanging out in New York with Daldry, Hall met his girlfriend, the writer Erin Cressida Wilson, then teaching creative writing at Duke University, resulting in a move to North Carolina.

I was at a loose end. But at that time, there was a fantastic video library at the university, so I used to stay home and watch all these videos of Bill Douglas and Terence Davies. And so, I was starting to think about my own childhood in the North East, through this frame of bumping into Bill Douglas films in North Carolina, and also trying to explain to people – both myself and my girlfriend – what a typical childhood was in the industrial area of the North East.[10]

Hall was aware of Ken Loach's achievements in social realism and had appreciated the 1960s Woodfall productions he had caught on television 'by accident' growing up.[11] But the poetic films of Douglas and Davies, specifically their respective 'Childhood' trilogies, which dealt with the film-makers' (often traumatic) experiences of growing up in Northern England, were new discoveries which moved him deeply – and form part of *Billy Elliot*'s dense web of cultural allusions. A scene in Douglas's *My Childhood* (1972), where the young Jamie warms his grandmother's hand on a heated teacup, finds an echo in the snowy sequence where Billy's friend Michael offers to warm his cold fingers. Similarly, the stilted Christmas dinner where Billy's father struggles to keep his emotions in check mirrors the disturbing scene in *Distant Voices, Still Lives* (1988) in which the family patriarch explodes with rage during a festive meal. Davies's affective use of music was also an inspiration, but less so the oblique narrative techniques that Hall now understood, through his late-blooming film education, as signifiers of a European art cinema tradition. In his introduction to the published screenplay of *Billy*

Publicity photograph for Bill Douglas's *My Ain Folk* (1973)

Elliot, he noted the irony of film-makers like Davies and Douglas – 'venerated by critics and institutions such as the BFI' – being 'drenched (Davies in particular) in popular culture'.[12]

Hall's observations chime with the scholarly recognition, around this time, of a British 'social art cinema' tradition using more exploratory forms to depict working-class experience,[13] but they also help elucidate the resulting film's relationship with its most discernible forebear. Ken Loach's *Kes* was based on Barry Hines's 1968 novel about a young boy called Billy Casper in a mining town briefly finding escape via the training of a bird of prey. The core idea and setting of *Billy Elliot* is undeniably like that of *Kes*, with the kestrel swapped for ballet classes. But there are also parallels between the respective Billy characters and their brothers, and some shared plot points. For example, both show their main character stealing a book. *Kes* also has a section where Billy Casper, running through his school to avoid being caught by his angry brother, creeps past a gymnasium where a girls' ballet class is taking place. The glances of a watchful teacher suggest he's very much not welcome.[14]

Publicity photograph for *Kes* (1969)

Just as Hall saw no reason to emulate the 'ascetic forms' of his cinematic inspirations,[15] so he rejected the gloomy determinism that has come to characterise Loach's career-long commitment to stories of oppression and hardship. After all, Hall's own story – of escape, of supportive mentors, of creative achievement – was a positive one, better suited to the strategies of magic realism he had already mastered in the *Jimmy Spud* radio play. In that, the main character undergoes training with the Archangel Gabriel to save his father from terminal cancer and seemingly does so in the end. However, Hall did not entirely view his approach as going against the Loachian grain, observing that, in his eyes, *Kes* transcended the strictures of social realism and was 'more playful than it's often given credit for'.[16] In this sense, placing Hall's work within a native kitchen-sink cycle is less useful than positioning it as part of an indigenous tradition of populist writing blurring registers of high and low. As Hall observes, 'Ealing films were made by very proper middle-class people but they deal with the warp and weave of real life.'[17]

Hall was also launching his writing career at the height of so-called 'in-yer-face-theatre', a tendency in 1990s British drama towards confrontation and shock, exemplified by playwrights such as Sarah Kane and Mark Ravenhill and strongly associated with Stephen Daldry's tenure as artistic director at the Royal Court Theatre.[18] Although nowhere near as extreme as the most famously provocative plays of this era – such as Kane's violent *Blasted* (1995) and Ravenhill's contentiously titled *Shopping and Fucking* (1996) – Hall's early writing for radio and theatre often finds humour in distasteful or shocking material. His black comedy *Cooking with Elvis* (first performed in 1998), arguably his most 'in-yer-face' work, was summarised, in a very dismissive profile of the author by the theatre critic Dominic Dromgoole, as being 'as broad as a comedy can get, piling sex on dirty jokes on cripples on naked men'.[19] Hall clearly revelled in the transgressive possibilities of child-related material, and *Billy Elliot*'s frequent profanities, and recognition of pre-pubescent sexuality, have a kinship with his contemporaneous

writing that explored the perspective of dying, traumatised, self-harming or sexually exploited children.[20] *Billy Elliot* arrived in close proximity to a cycle of child-oriented British movies that included *Ratcatcher* (1999), *Sweet Sixteen* (2002) and the *Harry Potter* films (2001–11), inviting speculation as to whether this was simply a happenstance spike within British cinema's long-standing engagement with childhood, or indicative of a deeper cultural and political concern with it during the Tony Blair era. Indeed, the prospective prime minister had established 'education, education, education' as one of his key priorities for government.[21]

However, a more formative influence on Hall's writerly aesthetic, perhaps even more so than the academic comprehension of history and form he gained as an English student at Cambridge, came through his teenage involvement with Tyneside's distinctive theatre culture of the 1980s. He recalls a well-resourced youth-theatre movement – overseen by full-time leaders whose remit was in part to educate and politicise young people through participatory methods. This resulted in Hall and his friends typically spending their Friday nights in 1984 in a 'sort of Kingdom Hall in Wallsend' doing self-devised work or adapting the Brecht play *Fear and Misery of the Third Reich* (1938) as a commentary on the reactionary forces at work during the time of the miners' strike; 'it didn't seem weird because it was just what you did, but in retrospect it was pretty amazing!'[22] Growing up in a working-class household, with parents who had never been to the theatre, and in an era and place where the decline of traditional industries made unemployment a given, Hall and his friends had grown up assuming 'culture' to belong elsewhere.

The scenario Hall describes, of being among 'quite an extraordinary group of teachers, writers, theatre-makers who were very much wanting to come to working-class places – places that were deprived of a lot of cultural opportunity',[23] finds a veiled expression in *Billy Elliot*:

Even we [Hall's company of peers] would have stuck our noses up at ballet, because it was the most aestheticised of the arts, whereas we were doing serious political theatre like Brecht would. But weirdly, through the working-class movements towards education, towards trying to find a cultural expression for working-class experience using the facilities and the funding of the state, we didn't experience the contradiction that is normally felt in working-class communities about art being other. We felt there was still suspicion from our parents or from our communities towards what we were doing. But we were working-class kids, so it didn't feel unnatural to tell that story.[24]

Hall also recalls there being seven producing theatre companies in Newcastle alone during this period, but one of the most significant for him was Live Theatre. Founded in 1973 and initially devising touring pieces to community audiences, by the early 1980s it had settled as a new-writing company based in Newcastle's quayside area, with a philosophy of presenting working-class stories to audiences in a demotic style.[25] They toured some of their plays to his school, and the work he saw by writers such as Tom Hadaway and C. P. Taylor impressed on him that one did not have to look far to find dramatic material.[26] In the mid-1980s, Max Roberts was appointed artistic director of Live Theatre, and – in the role for over thirty years – actively pursued writing commissions from writers both new and established, including Alan Plater, Julia Darling and Peter Straughan. Roberts commissioned Hall's first professional dramatic piece for Live, a ribald contribution to the anthology show *Twelve Tales of Tyneside* (1997) entitled 'Wittgenstein on Tyne', based on the true story of the philosopher's brief tenure as a hospital porter in a Newcastle hospital during World War II. At this time, Hall was given a writer-in-residence role at the theatre, which resulted in public rehearsed readings of some of his work-in-progress screenplays, including one of 'Dancer' – the original title for *Billy Elliot* – which, according to the author, 'tipped it into happening' because 'everybody could see how effective it was as a piece of drama in front of people'.[27]

However, Tyneside's theatrical scene was not the only creative influence on the young writer. Among his network of actor friends were those who had worked with Amber, a film and photography collective established in 1968 with the aim of documenting the region's working-class landscapes, communities and industries.[28] But it was the work of the Finnish-born Sirkka-Liisa Konttinen that held special significance. Hall's grandparents hailed from the working-class area of Newcastle that Konttinen had recorded while resident there in the 1970s, culminating in the *Byker* photography book and film (both 1983). *Byker* resonated as a personal, autobiographical response to a specific environment, Konttinen weaving her own memories and experiences into the accompanying text. Konttinen's *Step by Step* (1989) book – documenting the lives and aspirations of young girls going to dancing schools in the North Shields area – had another personal connection for Hall, as one of the main photographic subjects was a girl from his drama class at sixth-form college.

Emma Dowds, 1982 and *Connell-Brown Dancing School Dance Display at Terminus Club, 1982* from *Step by Step* (1989) (© Sirkka-Liisa Konttinen, courtesy AmberSide/L. Parker Stephenson Photographs, NY)

Hall would give copies of *Step by Step* to the production designers of *Billy Elliot* as a visual record of the world and time he had grown up in, but Konttinen and Amber's work also helped inspire a creative breakthrough:

> I had a sort of interregnum of ten years, wanting to do stuff with theatre, but not working out how to do it until I realised: oh, I should be doing what Sirkka did, and write about my backyard.[29] The more abstract or conceptual ideas that I'd been pursuing to write about had not really worked, and it wasn't until I got personal and autobiographical that it started to yield anything.[30]

Hall can remember clearly the moment when the idea of *Billy Elliot* came to him, at some point in 1995 while he was in North Carolina, and musing on ways to represent an idea of his childhood and the communities of the North East:

> I was in the bath one day and having this daydream about a kid in a tutu running down a back lane. I thought that was really weird, so I got out of the bath and wrote: well, he's a tutu-ed Geordie kid, and his dad must be a miner. I put it in a desk and forgot about it until a year later.[31]

In some interviews, Hall has also identified the image of a boy from a pit village jumping on his bed, as he used to do in his grandfather's house,[32] as one of his first inspirations. He also realised that the miners' strike, which took place from March 1984 to March 1985, was not only relatively unexplored in popular fiction, but also provided a helpfully bounded time-frame for a story about a young boy developing the requisite dancing skills, and overcoming setbacks, to make a successful ballet-school application feasible over the course of twelve months. Another visual influence was imagery, familiar from photographic records of the strike, of people in the street carrying on with their activities oblivious to the massing police in the background. As with the opening bedroom scene, and the coda showing an older Billy as a successful performer, the description of

Billy and his friend Debbie conversing in the street as they walk past riot police – one of the most cited aspects of the film's representation of childhood perspective – was present in Hall's very first draft. During the writing stage, Hall sought guidance from the Royal Ballet School and was pointed in the direction of the Barnsley-born Philip Mosley,[33] a professional dancer with a comparable backstory to Billy, although some other figures, such as the Plymouth-born but Hartlepool-bred Wayne Sleep[34] and the Durham-born classical baritone Thomas Allen,[35] have made claims to be the primary inspiration.

Hall pitched his 'Dancer' idea to the BBC's head of Single Drama, George Faber, who agreed to back it, but a slate of other commitments meant that it took a further year for Hall to deliver the first script. The prospect of a northern, working-class setting, and the unfashionable topic of the miners' strike, allegedly gave the broadcaster some pause for thought, and neither did it make for an easy fit with BBC Films' attempts to 'establish itself as an independent company and a maker of more ambitious cinematic films',[36] following the success of *Mrs Brown* (1997). Ultimately, BBC Films invested about £800,000 – half of which was for television rights (this would pay dividends with extremely high ratings for its eventual broadcast)[37] and half for equity, in keeping with its policy of spreading its £10 million budget across a range of projects.[38] The eventual success of *Billy Elliot* validated BBC Films' stated commitment to fostering and retaining existing talent within the indigenous film industry. It also demonstrated that the BBC and ITV, as per the stipulation of the 1990 Broadcasting Act, had to source at least a quarter of their output from independent companies, and how public service broadcasters could boost the independent production sector by providing early-stage development and investment to 'facilitate the co-production of films which might not otherwise get made'.[39]

At the BBC, Tessa Ross, then an independent commissioning executive for drama, guided Hall to find an independent production company to develop the project, at the time earmarked as a likely TV production. Greg Brenman, then head of drama at Tiger Aspect, remembers Ross brokering a meeting between him and Hall:

I met him, and literally there was one side of A4 telling the story of this project called 'Dancer'. And we loved it. He chose to come with us, and over the course of two, maybe three years, we developed the script with him. The first draft was really, really good.[40]

'Dancer' was mentioned in a *Screen International* report of November 1997 as one of the projects on Tiger Aspect's slate under Brenman's wing, in which the chairman Peter Bennett-Jones described the company's newfound film production drive as 'modest but clear: we're looking to do relatively small-budgeted, British-based films as an extension of the relationships we already have with talent'.[41] 'Dancer' would be their second after the successful Harry Enfield vehicle *Kevin & Perry Go Large* (2000). The development of Hall's script was guided by Greg Brenman and Tessa Ross at the BBC, and Roanna Benn, script editor at Tiger Aspect. The most significant change, suggested by Benn, was the decision to kill off the character of Billy's mother, to focus attention on the boy's relationship with his brother and father. She recalls:

The first draft came in and it was in such fantastic shape, although we felt that the script would be stronger still if it could have even more emotional depth. By making this change, Lee was able to explore the themes of loss and grief which he is so interested in and writes about so brilliantly. Billy's fury and incomprehension about his mum's death powers him through the film. And despite Dad maintaining that ballet is the wrong thing to be involved in for a boy from his background, we know his resistance is also about his fear of losing Billy, who is the deep connection to his lost wife.[42]

For Hall, the dead mother provided an 'emblem of this loss that runs through the whole piece',[43] but this intervention by Benn also exemplifies how the development process not only enhanced the film structurally and tonally but also helped Hall to refine his authorial voice.

Tiger Aspect had a development deal with Working Title, arguably one of the most prominent UK film (and later television) production companies since its inception in 1983. Brenman says:

The reason we had that deal was because one of the directors of Tiger Aspect was Rowan Atkinson, and so [Working Title] were keen to get comedy films out of our company, but none materialised at the time. And so, we asked them to look at Billy Elliot. They took a look and said: OK, we can put this through the deal.[44]

At Working Title, the script was received enthusiastically by production executive Jon Finn, who was setting up the company's low-budget WT² offshoot with Natascha Wharton and would take a hands-on production role on both the film and its eventual theatrical version. Finn's connection with the story was instantaneous and deeply felt:

It's the only script that ever made me cry, before or since, because it's set in the North East. All my family were miners, and we ended up shooting it in Easington, which was the last place my grandad worked. I can still remember sitting in bed, reading it one night, and crying.[45]

As the two key North Easterners on the creative team, Hall and Finn would often be called upon to sense-check for local authenticity; for example, supporting the decision to cast the Scottish actor Gary Lewis in the role of Billy's father, using his own Glaswegian accent, because they could give first-hand evidence of some Scots migrants working in the East Durham coalfields.

For Finn, the story not only encapsulated the deep, visceral hatred of Thatcher that he and many in North East England still felt with respect to the miners' strike, but also the sense of isolation felt by those – like him, like Hall – who deviated in some way from the norms of their home environment.

It managed to capture the feeling of not belonging that so many people have. The idea that you can love where you live, but you can't live there, because that world doesn't allow for you, is so powerful. It's exactly what I felt about Newcastle: I love it, but I felt like a fucking alien.[46]

Like Hall, like young Billy, Finn inevitably gravitated to London, where he remembers being judged and belittled because of his Tyneside accent. This is corroborated in Geoffrey Macnab's historical account of the British film industry, which notes Finn's role in the 'runaway box-office hit *Billy Elliot*' in tandem with an aside about his former, low-profile activity as company receptionist, and how 'some remember visitors struggling to understand his Geordie accent'.[47] If this classist anecdote implies a Billy-type story of underdog victory against the odds, it also speaks to the considerable achievement of the film's uncompromising commitment to regional dialect.

The lower budgets afforded to films produced by the WT² subsidiary – there was a $5 million limit for the purpose of creating 'low-budget films that people want to go and see'[48] – was intended to support riskier, less starry and polished fare, and the work of new writers. When Tim Bevan and Eric Fellner defined its remit in 2000 as the 'three H's' of 'heart, humour and horror',[49] there was an implicit alignment of the first two with indigenous traditions of social realism and television comedy. Aside from *Billy Elliot*, their output would include *Inside I'm Dancing* (2004), *Ali G Indahouse* (2002) and *Shaun of the Dead* (2004). As Nathan Townsend has observed in his scholarly analysis of the short-lived WT² experiment (which effectively ended around 2006 when the division was folded back into Working Title), the subsidiary was positioned a little precariously between 'forces of the national and the transitional'.[50] This is exemplified in several ways by *Billy Elliot*, its most successful film. As with other WT² projects, it was a co-production among UK operators, but it was financed and distributed by global multimedia conglomerates. If there was scope for the film to draw upon a native social-realist tradition of representational extension – deviating considerably from the Richard Curtis template in its depiction of regionality, class and political history – there was perhaps a mindfulness of the global orientation of the parent companies. Hence, the shaping of WT² films around 'universalistic triumph-over-adversity narratives' gave limited scope for social commentary.[51]

Such sweeping assessments inevitably jar with the retrospective accounts of the project's evolution given by the film's creators, such as Jon Finn, who emphasises the passion involved, and the hard-won autonomy of the team:

> It generally gets forgotten that it was tough as hell to make, no one really wanted it, no one was 100% convinced, and it was questioned all the way through. For me it was somewhere to channel my anger and joy. It's actually the way of most films, but it definitely felt like us against the world.[52]

Where recollections do seem to vary is over the arm's-length involvement of Working Title's co-chairs. While Finn does not remember Bevan and Fellner making any visits to the set, some journalists were invited to Shepperton Studios (in London) during filming to talk with Bevan and Fellner about 'Dancer' and the WT² strategy for promoting emerging British writers, directors and producers. In an article in the *Evening Standard* before the film came out, one journalist reported that it was a 'crucial release' for the company and that 'expectations are high'[53] – a sentiment slightly at odds with a post-release consensus that its success was yet another unheralded 'fluke'[54] or 'surprise'[55] for the British film industry. There was soon talk in the trade press about an 'unseemly scramble to claim credit for its success',[56] understandable given the complex parentage, with Tiger Aspect's chair Bennett-Jones breaking rank to criticise other partners in the film for playing down his company's involvement.[57]

An in-depth article on the film's production that ran in *Variety* in October 2000 cited an 'exec close to the project' saying that 'whatever anyone claims now, none of us, nobody in the world, really believed in this movie apart from Daldry and Finn'.[58] For his part, Finn believes it may have never been made without Stephen Daldry's involvement, given that the script had been turned down by numerous potential directors. A leading light of the 1990s theatre scene, Daldry played a key role in the development of new writing as

Stephen Daldry on the set of Billy Elliot

artistic director of the Royal Court between 1992 and 1998, and in 1997 struck a 'first look' deal with Working Title, giving the director an autonomous development fund to work on projects for the company. By this time, Finn had set up a scriptwriting competition with the Jermyn Foundation for young authors, offering an £80,000 budget for the completion of a short film. Daldry would be both a judge and the film's director, which resulted in him using Tim Clague's script to make *Eight* (1998), about an eight-year-old boy from Liverpool who moves away from home with his mother. With its child perspective, and its insinuation that the boy's father has perished in the 1989 Hillsborough disaster, *Eight* raised a curtain on thematic ideas that would dominate *Billy Elliot*, which was made using many of the same crew.[59] Although in interviews he tended to brush off the notion of a personal investment in the *Billy Elliot* story, he recalled putting on a play in a pit village outside Doncaster during the time of the miners' strike concerning the role of women in the dispute.[60]

The veteran cinematographer Brian Tufano was recommended to Daldry by Danny Boyle as the ideal director of photography for a debut film, not least because of his work on all Boyle's films to date at that point. With a career stretching back to the late 1960s, and straddling both film and television, Tufano considered himself a specialist in working with rookie directors on limited budgets. For the director Saul Metzstein, who also worked with him as a first-time director, Tufano's work was characterised by a synthesis of two seemingly different impulses: the small-scale intimacy of kitchen-sink drama and the 'more elaborate stylized technique' of grander, commercially oriented cinema.[61] Daldry was encouraged by Tufano's philosophy of 'using the whole frame rather than following the action',[62] to avoid any 'overblown use of the camera',[63] moving it only when essential to the narrative, in the fashion of Mike Leigh's films. Daldry also brought from his established circle of contacts the composer Stephen Warbeck, with whom he had worked in the theatre since the 1980s. Over the six months that Daldry and Hall undertook script revisions, the director helped to draw out the material's 'connections to melodrama and musicals',[64] for example finessing the 'tough love' of Mrs Wilkinson, and ramping up the emotional impact of Billy's thawing relationship with his father.

At the casting stage, Julie Walters – in the role of the dancing instructor Mrs Wilkinson – was the obligatory 'name' required for commercial viability, even though her film career (if not her television fame) had dwindled slightly since her breakthrough hit playing a mature working-class university student in *Educating Rita* (1983).[65] A greater challenge was finding the right child for the main part, a boy who could not only act and dance, but was 'a genuine northern lad' with the right accent,[66] and most definitely not a polished 'stage school kid'.[67] The intensive scouring of dance schools, youth clubs and even skateboarding parks, and the auditioning of two thousand children, had failed to provide a 'eureka' moment.

The extended search for the right Billy led to an escalation of the film's budget, which resulted in an application being made to Arts Council England, who awarded £850,000 of National Lottery funding in July 1999.[68] As film scholar James Caterer has discovered, via confirmation by the Arts Council officer responsible for

approving the *Billy Elliot* application, one strategy of success was to 'highlight the project's relevance to key policy directions of the day'.[69] Following the Culture Secretary Chris Smith's advocacy of the arts and sports as 'weapons in the fight against social exclusion', it made sense for the Council to respond warmly to the film's insinuation of 'industrial rags-to-cultural riches'.[70]

Playing a vital role in the casting of Billy was Peter Darling, recruited to the film in the role of choreographer. Darling's background was as a performer in physical theatre, including a stint with Lloyd Newson's innovative DV8 Physical Theatre company. DV8 were known for productions like their pub-set *Enter Achilles* (1995), a deconstruction of contemporary masculinity, in which dancers move dextrously with beer glasses and footballs, anticipating the way that Billy discovers the balletic possibilities of the boxing ring. Darling had only recently turned to choreography when he was approached by Daldry, after the director saw his work on a National Theatre production of *Oh What a Lovely War*. Despite not having ballet training himself, Darling realised that Hall's script chimed with his interest in men and movement, and in dance being a broad spectrum; furthermore, Newson – whom he considered his mentor – had instilled in him the idea that 'everything should be real in order for the stakes to be really high'.[71]

According to Darling, the initial candidate for the Billy part was a 'complete non-dancer', but he had footballing skills that were used to formulate the routine intended to be the character's final dance for his father, which convinces him to support his son's talent. However, the limitations of the performer's football-centric movements supported the case that the actor really needed to be an expressive dancer. The casting director was then asked to go back through the audition tapes to see if such a person had been missed, which led to the discovery of twelve-year-old Jamie Bell, who attended seven day-long sessions before being offered the part. For Darling, it was important to veer the film away from any sentimentality towards the figure of the plucky amateur, and thus to distinguish the story from the likes of *The Full Monty*, which located comedy and pathos in the prospect of untrained performers awkwardly but gamely devising a stripping routine to music: 'A sense of British amateurism wouldn't really cut it. British people love the trier, and we shy back from celebrating excellence, in a way that Americans do. What Stephen [Daldry], myself and Lee [Hall] were chasing was some kind of midway.'[72]

Unsurprisingly, around the time of the film's release, there was substantial press interest in the 'remarkable similarities between the stories of Billy and Jamie himself'.[73] Bell came from a working-class background in Billingham, about fifteen miles south of the film's implied location of Easington, and like Billy from a single-parent family (his parents divorced before he was born). According to assorted press reports, Bell had developed an interest in dance at the age of six and subsequently took up dancing and then acting classes. He had performed locally in pantomimes and shows, toured nationally with the National Youth Music Theatre, and had won competitions in tap solo, and in song and dance. Although Bell possibly met Darling's ideal of the 'midway' point between plucky amateurism and stage-school slickness, having had some experience of 'smiley-face, sparkly-costume kind of things',[74] the promotional materials for the film tended to play down his prior acting experience. Daldry told one interviewer that the boy had 'not acted before'[75] –

which was true for the cinema, if not the stage – and the film's press pack relayed the director's belief that 'real life similarities to his film character were key', and that 'if you can get a child to act truthfully it is incredibly powerful and very moving'.[76] Working with Bell on the dance sequences prior to filming, Darling was impressed with his skills of mimicry, and his instinctive rhythm: 'I could ask him to take one step and play with it, to turn the rhythm, or to accent a rhythm'.[77]

Having been cast at the end of June 1999, Bell embarked on an eight-week training period, working with Darling to shape the dance routines, before shooting began on 23 August on location in North East England. Billy's neighbourhood is named as the fictional Everington, but most of the outdoor scenes were filmed in Easington Colliery, a village that evolved out of the sinking of the Easington pit at the turn of the twentieth century (and not to be confused with the more established Easington Village nearby). With a sleight-of-hand not uncommon for production teams prioritising visual interest over geographical accuracy, some 'Everington' scenes were also filmed in nearby Seaham and Dawdon, such as the evocative shots of Billy walking or dancing through the streets against the backdrop of a vast expanse of sea, while Lynemouth Colliery (decommissioned in 1994) in Northumberland was utilised for the mining scenes. Easington Colliery had been the location of one of the last surviving pits of East Durham, but had closed in 1993, its distinguishing wheel quickly removed and its site grassed over – exemplary for Hall of how 'a whole industry had been physically erased in 10 years'.[78] Even before its *Billy Elliot* fame, the area had become a byword for social decay, described by one visiting journalist in 2000 as the 'fourth-most deprived local authority area in Britain in terms of health, housing, education and life expectancy'. This was a place with 'boarded-up buildings and disillusioned, hard-drinking, unemployed ex-miners',[79] not to mention an endemic drug problem, which led the production team to observe that 'people come and go scoring drugs' in the street where Billy was shown to live.[80]

Police and striking miners clash in Easington, 24 August 1984 (NCJ Archive/Mirrorpix/Getty Images)

The pit-workers of Easington Colliery had been the first in the North East to walk out on strike, following the resolution of the Durham NUM executive on 9 March 1984,[81] and the resulting clashes led to the first ever deployment of riot police in the region.[82] The production team have confessed to some naivety in their casting of local people, including many ex-miners, as extras for sequences of violent clashes between picketers and police, not anticipating that many would refuse to play the latter, or find the prospect triggering. For producer Jon Finn, this was a 'real lesson in going into someone's community and restaging one of its most traumatic moments'.[83] *Billy Elliot* was also in danger of perpetuating negative stereotypes about an area that was already the 'default setting for an ailing pit village', as featured in numerous film and television productions of the 1990s, including the 1984-set episode of *Our Friends in the North* (1996).[84]

There were other setbacks to overcome. As an inexperienced director, Daldry was still finding his feet with the practicalities and protocols of film shoots. The experienced Tufano was 'not the quickest' in his set-ups,[85] although was resourceful when a freak

windstorm affecting drapes necessitated the overhaul of lighting for the pivotal 'I Love to Boogie' dance sequence; rehearsed over three weeks, and allocated a full day's shoot, the actors only had 'less than 30 minutes' to perform it.[86] With studio work for interior scenes completed at Shepperton, the shoot finished on 13 October. In post-production, some scenes were moved around, cut altogether or had 'off face' dialogue added,[87] while wrangling continued to secure rights for the pop music selected for the soundtrack.

Despite some positive test screenings, Daldry and Hall harboured doubts about the merits of the film. The producer Finn was told by a prominent figure within the British film industry that they'd succeeded in making a film for only 'faggots and old women'.[88] However, its screening, as 'Dancer', in the Directors' Fortnight selection of the Cannes Film Festival on 19 May 2000 was prompting ovations, gushing reviews ('a feel-good factor that registers off the scale')[89] and an overcome Elton John being 'taken from the theatre on a stretcher'.[90] By now, the film had also found a strong personal advocate in Stacey Snider, the chairman of Universal Pictures,[91] who chose it to launch to the US market their new specialist division Universal Focus, geared towards relatable films benefitting from a press-driven, slow-burn, word-of-mouth campaign.[92] There was just one final hurdle to overcome before the UK release date of 29 September: potential market confusion with Lars von Trier's Palme d'Or-winning *Dancer in the Dark* (2000), another experiment in combining a realist aesthetic with the tropes of Hollywood musicals and melodrama.

With 'Raising Billy Elliot' briefly in contention, the eventual title was explained in a press release as a means to draw attention to Bell's performance and to generate more 'across-the-board-appeal'.[93] Always intended by Hall as a 'John Doe' symbol of ordinariness, *Billy Elliot* brought together a common surname in North East England and the diminutive form of an everyday UK first name, albeit with a fine British social-realist cinematic pedigree via the main characters of *Billy Liar* (1963) and *Kes*.[94] But if the title has an appropriately proletarian quality, it also focuses attention on individual, exceptional achievement, in contrast with the more workman-like qualities of 'Dancer'. Still, it is difficult to conceive of 'Dancer' achieving the adjectival status that the final title would quickly gain, and in its own way *Billy Elliot* has a kind of vernacular musicality that suits the film well, as the following chapter will demonstrate.

2 Dancer: *Billy Elliot* by Numbers

Billy Elliot is not a musical. None of the characters break into song, and only a few of them dance. Nor – despite its broad nexus of debts and references to movies involving physical movement, from Powell and Pressburger's *The Red Shoes* (1948) to Adrian Lyne's *Flashdance* (1983) – can it be really categorised as a dance film. Still, the producer Jon Finn's definition of it as a 'musical trying to escape from a Ken Loach film'[95] has some legitimacy, particularly considering its eventual transformation into a stage musical. Although the film doesn't exactly have self-contained 'numbers' as such, its use of pop and classically scored music is at times reminiscent of musicals, and there are moments of dance performance that are inspired by visual and thematic tropes from the Hollywood musical tradition.

Cosmic dancer

Following a title card against a black screen identifying the setting as 'Durham Coalfield, North East England, 1984', *Billy Elliot* begins with a close-up of a record player, and a pan upwards to show young hands removing the vinyl of the T. Rex *Electric Warrior* album (1971) from its sleeve and – very deliberately – positioning it on the turntable, and setting the stylus in place; initially wrongly, as evidenced by a blast of the backwards guitar that concludes the song 'Cosmic Dancer', but then at the rightful beginning point. As the film starts, T. Rex's Marc Bolan sings the narratively appropriate words 'I was

dancing when I was twelve'. There is a cut to a series of shots showing a smiling, red-faced boy in a yellow vest and red/green gymnastic shorts against a repeated-sunburst wallpaper pattern bouncing joyfully in slow motion in and out of the frame. It takes a full minute of these fragmented glimpses before we are given a wide perspective that takes in the boy's full body, now meeting our gaze directly as he tumbles acrobatically against a widescreen expansion of the wallpaper backdrop that draws attention to its own heightened artifice.

Viewers familiar with *Kes* will no doubt recognise the establishment here – and in the subsequent scenes of the Elliot household and the neighbouring streets – of a comparable visual and thematic dialectic between images of 'freedom, creativity and agency, and those of imprisonment, conformity and hopeless drudgery'.[96] Through resources of set design, framing, camerawork and editing, the film juxtaposes cramped sites of tightly framed restriction – home, school, the mine, the neighbourhood under the repressive surveillance and control of the police – with places of potential for Billy's creative imagination: the hall where dancing classes take place, the streets and eventually the London theatre of the future. Our gaze is drawn towards Billy's body and its possibility for grace. The disembodied hand we see operating the record player is expressive enough to convey, through micro-gestures of flattening and clenching, Billy's anticipatory mood and also his anxiety about treating the apparatus with care. A reasonable concern, given that, in a subsequent scene, his volatile brother – the record's owner – will accuse him of damaging it. The isolation of body parts here loosely evokes the work of the choreographer Bob Fosse, but Peter Darling also took inspiration from experimental dance television productions, including one he remembers, likely in the BBC/Arts Council England's *Dance for the Camera* strand (1994–2001), involving, in his words, 'just two fingers dancing on a sofa', which gave him the realisation that 'it was the tight close-up of detail in solo dances that would deliver something you couldn't achieve in the theatre'.⁹⁷ In preparation for *Billy Elliot*, Darling had also been directed to look at Rosemary Lee's choreography for *Boy* (1996), a short dance film exploring the 'physical and emotional qualities' of a young boy's experience as he makes movements on a beach, through cinematic devices of sound and editing, including implied doubling – the boy dancing with a version of himself – and close-ups of hand gestures.⁹⁸

The inclusion of a literal and tactile 'needle drop' – the term now used routinely to describe the strategic synchronisation of film image and popular music – and Billy's seeming acknowledgment of

Marc Bolan (Estate of Keith Morris/Redferns/Getty Images)

the audience as he bounces, through a direct gaze at the camera, can be understood in relation to Hall's desire to 'ironise this social-realist world' and be 'very tongue in cheek about where the strings are being pulled'.[99] Billy's selection of 'Cosmic Dancer' also had very personal associations for Hall, who remembers buying a 'best of T. Rex' compilation in a branch of W. H. Smith in Newcastle when he was twelve.[100] He originally constructed the entire *Billy Elliot* story around Marc Bolan songs,[101] but the conceptual purity of the idea was compromised by knotty rights entanglements, resulting in other 1970s pop songs being used in addition to the five Bolan tracks that were secured.

During the film's production, the inclusion of anachronistic music – *Electric Warrior* was released twelve years before 1983, thus was older than Billy himself – was debated, but Hall clung

42 | BFI FILM CLASSICS

Michael Clark (Jack Mitchell/Getty Images)

to the argument that people 'don't only listen to what's happening, the latest thing'.[102] Both Bolan and *Electric Warrior*, his calculated move towards a more commercial sound following a more countercultural period, are recognised as foundational for the early 1970s glam-rock movement, which carried signifiers of gender-bending relevant to *Billy Elliot*'s thematic interests, but also, as music scholar Philip Auslander puts it, emphasised 'accessibility and fun', celebrating performance aspects of spectacle and theatricality.[103]

Cosmic Dancer had also been famously set to movement by the groundbreaking dancer and choreographer Michael Clark,[104] known for his cross-media associations with musicians, costumiers and film-makers in the 1980s and 1990s. It was included in a touring show that Hall remembers seeing in Newcastle in the early 1990s and being profoundly taken with,[105] and a 1985 television recording of the routine shows us a gliding, limb-curving Clark dressed in a long, flowing yellow dress.

A cutaway from Billy's bedroom takes us to him entering a cramped kitchen busily overrun with food and washing items, the Bolan track continuing as he prepares his grandmother's breakfast tray of eggs, toast and tablets in a clearly familiar but playfully ragged routine. Incorporating skilful toast-catching and a sporty heading of a dangling plastic bag, the sequence has a kinship with one of the best-remembered musical routines of British television comedy:

Eric Morecambe and Ernie Wise's 'Breakfast Sketch' of 1976 from their long-running BBC series, where they perform an amusing dance, choreographed to the music of David Rose's 'The Stripper' (1962), involving kitchen utensils and food items. Whether a conscious homage or not, the sequence positions *Billy Elliot* in a lineage of popular art that locates musicality even in the most unexpected or mundane environments. Once Billy realises that his grandmother is not in her bed, he races out through his yard and into the back lane – with shaky and low-angle camerawork conveying his concern – until he locates her in an area of scrubland in a confused state. As he guides her back home, the camera pans up to observe policemen with riot shields and vans assembling on a road overhead.

From the outset, the film presents the Elliots as a family in disarray. The mother has passed away, the father and older son are at loggerheads over Tony's aggressive picketing, and both Billy and Tony are undertaking housework and caring roles traditionally classified as feminine, including looking after a grandmother with signs of dementia. Meanwhile, the gathering of policemen and vehicles, seen in the background of multiple scenes, conveys the siege-like conditions in Everington and the looming threat of violence. Their presence in the distance or on the edge of the frame in various sequences was also, as the director Daldry explained in the film's DVD commentary, a means to reduce the likelihood of the miners'-strike context being minimised by wary financiers. The tonal shift, from the opening suggestion of childish glee to the articulation of both family and societal disruption, finds accommodation in the curious register of 'Cosmic Dancer'. As the musician and writer Bob Stanley observes, the song 'could be a fey boast', yet such are the archaic elements of the lyric and the impact of the melancholic string scoring, it seems to be 'as much about loss, absence, and regret'.[106]

As if to insinuate Billy's innate sensitivity to music, this opening sequence is artfully edited to match sound and image, with locations changing in step with lyrical lines, and some bodily movements aligned with aspects of the song's production. For instance, Billy gallops to reach his grandmother to the accompaniment of an insistent two-note string motif, and the police in the distance appear to the sound of militaristic drum fill. The song ends abruptly through a 'needle scratch' which reveals that Tony has been listening to it on headphones, while smoking a joint, in the bedroom he shares with Billy. The abrasive impact of the skipping needle here establishes the film's consistent device of unsettling lurches, whether in the form of sudden tonal shifts, or through hard stops to musical 'numbers' that undercut the pleasures, for both the characters and audience, of escapist musical fantasy.

The 'mother' theme

In a subsequent scene sketching out the Elliot family dynamics, and his father's antipathy to music – whether for reasons of sentiment, mood or perhaps a suspicion of what it might suggest about his son – Billy repeatedly picks out a four-note melody on an upright piano: A, D, A (octave higher) and E. His noodling irritates his granite-faced father, who commands him to stop, but Billy maintains that 'Mam would have let us', and a camera pan upwards to family photographs on top of the instrument accentuates the motif's association with his dead mother – and it will duly recur on Warbeck's orchestral score at key points, most prominently when Billy has a vision of her in his kitchen. The four-note motif has a rising and falling curve that is the musical equivalent of one of Billy's flying leaps, but the holding of the notes together implies a suspended chord, which has the emotive effect of indeterminacy and irresolution, but also possibility.

The film's composer Stephen Warbeck recalls the creative decision to imagine that Billy was picking out the notes of a melody that his mother used to play on an instrument left untuned since her death:

The 'mother' theme, which would then be used in different parts of the film, would become a theme of loss, but also of aspiring to something outside the immediate realities of his life. It suggests that there is a door or portal open to that universe of self-expression. It asks a question and doesn't tell you how it should resolve but suggests that the piece will go on somewhere else.[107]

From a command to stop playing, the father progresses, in this scene, to a firm slam of the lid, and later he destroys the piano for firewood, the instrument issuing sustained, discordant clangs as he strains to hammer it. These anguished sounds convey the emotions that a grieving, struggling father cannot articulate in words or actions, but also the tragedy of what Warbeck describes as one of the most

emotive aspects of the story, the idea of a 'young person having this talent or this passion, and doors being shut in their face; the fact that people's potential, in so many circumstances, is never realized'.[108]

However, the latent potential of the 'mother' theme to evolve into something meaningful – which occurs when Warbeck's score develops it further – can also be read in relation to Richard Dyer's writing on how the musical genre embodies the 'utopian' possibilities of entertainment. Dyer suggests that the musical, in providing imagery (and sounds) of escape, can project the sense that 'things could be better, that something other than what is can be imagined and maybe realised'.[109] Again, *Billy Elliot* may not be a musical per se, but Billy's tentative piano-playing, like his first exploratory dance movements, are a portal of sorts to a new world of possibility, a utopian solution, in Dyer's terms, to the poverty – both financial and of the imagination – characterising the Elliot family when we first meet them.

The sun'll come out tomorrow

As the world-weary dance teacher Mrs Wilkinson, first seen in the boxing hall distractedly flicking through a newspaper as she delivers instructions to her pupils, Julie Walters gives one of the film's most renowned line deliveries, in the form of a command to her equally jaded accompanist. 'Right, Mr Braithwaite,' she says, looking off-screen right, 'The Sun'll Come Out Tomorrow'. A small pause, and a well-timed head-turn to the right – 'Fat chance' – as she exits the frame, in the manner of a comedian triumphantly throwing down a microphone. We may fairly assume she's referring to one of the key lyrics of the song known as 'Tomorrow', associated with the heroine of the musical *Annie*, and its 1982 film adaptation. The gag of course being that the optimistic sentiment of the number sung by the orphan Annie is somewhat contrary to Mrs Wilkinson's current world-view. Yet there is another sly joke at work here, which is that the number Mr Braithwaite launches into is definitely not 'Tomorrow', but instead a rather plodding, simple and functionally

nondescript piece, a backdrop for Billy to impress the teacher with his ability to hold his leg in position.

The non-appearance of 'Tomorrow' only emphasises the status of the boxing hall as a place of potential nonconformity, through the happenstance of the ballet and boxing classes sharing the same space.[110] The bleeding through of the ballet music to the boxing ring inspires Billy to flail theatrically around his opponent, and thereafter to treat a punchbag like a dancing partner. A place where odd but transformative things can occur, the boxing hall is clearly a loose metaphor for Hall's personal experience of life-changing theatrical activities in civic spaces not unlike this. The cinematographer Brian Trufano described Daldry's brief as wanting the scenes here to have a 'lighter quality, a kind of heightened realism'.[111] The hall's liberatory qualities are denoted by its predominantly blue decoration and its relative expansiveness, amplified by mirrors that sometimes create doubling effects, and it also offers an early stage for Billy to perform,

watched – with very different reactions – by his father, Debbie and the other ballet girls, and his soon-to-be teacher.

The boxing-hall-as-theatre notion allows for the identification of another, perhaps unexpected, mentor: the boxing instructor identified in the credits as George Watson, who provides a commentary on Billy's atrocious ring technique:

Jesus Christ, Billy Elliot, you're a disgrace to them gloves, your father and the traditions of this boxing hall. You owe us fifty pence. [Addressing Mr Braithwaite, the pianist] How! Liberace, will you give it a rest!

George's speech has more flowing cadence than the terse, staccato dialogue that otherwise dominates the film, even if it is no less profane. A fellow miner and friend to Billy's father, the character's alignment with traditional notions of masculinity is evident in the dismissive reference here to the (famously flamboyant) pianist and singer Liberace, and also in his description of Billy's boxing-ring prancing as resembling a 'fanny in a fit': a colloquial phrase with likely sexual overtones. This sequence hinges on a transfer of keys between George and Mrs Wilkinson, but also on a contrapuntal clash between their respective voices: not just between registers of masculine and feminine, but of colloquial speech against highfalutin French ballet terms ('port de bras' and so on), the low versus the high.

However, both characters, in their different fashion, have a mastery of timing, which we witness Billy developing as the film progresses. The comedy of *Billy Elliot* is not that of humorous incidents or pay-offs, or of jokes per se, but mostly of reaction. Sometimes this takes the form of tension-deflating responses, as with Billy's deadpan 'Nah, you're alright' reaction to Debbie offering to show him her 'fanny', but he also plays the faux-innocent comedy sidekick to Mrs Wilkinson's revelation that she's been thinking about the Royal Ballet School: 'Aren't you a bit old, miss?' In the same scene, he implores her not to 'lose her blob', a curious coinage conveying Billy's nascent skills of invention. Hall has described his approach to humour in both Shakespearean and Brechtian terms, in the sense of fusing the tragic and comedic, but also allowing for a laugh to follow a gut punch, or vice versa. Billy's relationship to his father follows a trajectory from the dad's humourless response to his son's behaviour to a deadpan joke in response to Billy's admission of being scared at the prospect of going to ballet school: 'Are you kidding? We've let out your room'.

Top hat, white tie and tails

Having been encouraged by Mrs Wilkinson to continue with his ballet classes, Billy absent-mindedly taps, kicks and swings a big stick like a dancer's cane, to the sound of Fred Astaire singing

'Top Hat, White Tie and Tails', followed by a full-screen excerpt from its source movie *Top Hat* (1935). We see Astaire, the epitome of the poised performer, leading a group of about twenty identically dressed male dancers, and giving a smiling acknowledgment of the camera in an implicit kinship with Billy in the opening sequence. A slow dissolve leaves the men superimposed for a second or two over a long-shot composition of Billy and his grandmother on a grassy landscape, with two industrial towers in the distance – roughly at the height of the men's gloves, as if an alternative cane for them. The screen is dominated however by looming, dark-grey clouds with the

appropriate silver hue for cinema projection. As Astaire's troupe disappears, Billy leads his grandmother from the left to the right of the screen, as she reminisces about watching Astaire at the Palace picture house and 'dancing around the front room like lunatics'.

As Cynthia Weber has observed, the film has established, through the absence of Billy's mother and the mental and physical wanderings of his grandmother, 'death and senility in the places where the feminine ought to be',[112] which may explain his requirement to fulfil stereotypically 'female' roles of caring and cooking for his family. According to this reading, Billy's dancing proclivities precipitate a crisis of masculinity, at least one for his brother and father. For Weber, the *Top Hat* superimposition 'narratively places Astaire's dancing body and (by idealistic identification) Billy's dancing body into a space that masculinizes, heterosexualizes, and utopianizes dance'.[113] The following shots clarify that Billy is visiting a graveyard overlooked by industrial works,[114] a site thus suggestive of depletion and termination at both the levels of traditional industry and Billy's own family situation, with Billy posited as the potential agent of recuperation.

In a succinct signifier of the societal fractures that will be accelerated by pit closures in towns like Everington/Easington, Billy discovers that his mother's grave has been vandalised with beer

cans and spray paint. This upsetting image, accompanied here by a melancholic piano melody, connects the film with Tony Harrison's powerful state-of-the-nation poem 'V', published in 1985, describing his discovery of graffiti on tombstones, including those of his parents, in a Leeds cemetery. The football-related desecrations Harrison sees include repeated 'v's that prompt him, in one stanza, to locate the personification of 'us and them' class warfare as the dispute between 'Coal Board MacGregor and the NUM' – in other words, between Ian MacGregor, then head of the NCB, and the striking National Union of Mineworkers.[115]

Three Bolan songs

In between the Bolan songs that bookend the film, are three – 'Get It On' (1971), 'Children of the Revolution' (1972) and 'I Love to Boogie' (1976) – that are utilised in a montage-like fashion to advance the plot, smooth over some temporal and geographical jumps, and to sketch out Billy's relationship respectively with Michael, Debbie and Mrs Wilkinson. These three cheerful, strident songs can be summarised in turn as self-aware expressions of sexual energy, countercultural confidence and sheer joy in dance. While they lend momentum and energy to these scenes, the songs also generate some subtle discordances and transgressions. 'Get It On', with its

overtly libidinous lyrics like 'you're dirty, sweet and you're my girl', accompanies school scenes of Billy being longingly gazed upon by Michael in a classroom, Billy puffing out his chest in the mirror and then Michael quizzing Billy about his clothing requirements for dance classes – he reckons Billy would look 'wicked' in a tutu – while they take a cross-country run shortcut via a flooded aqueduct. The music spills over into a new sequence of Billy approaching a mobile library to source a book about ballet, the gatekeeping librarian – in one of the many allusions to *Kes* – bringing both the song and his right to borrow this 'adult' book to a dead halt. But it comes back with the sudden appearance through the window of a picketer mooning at pursuing policemen, which offers him the chance to steal it, rather neatly at the point where Bolan intones the line 'take me'. There follows, as the music fades out, overhead shots of the boxing-club staircase, with Billy looking upwards towards flurrying ballerinas. Accordingly, the 'Get It On' sequence cycles through a series of child gazes – Michael at Billy, Billy at himself, Billy at the ballerinas – and adult expressions of supposed safeguarding (the librarian) and physicality (the mooner), but ultimately, thanks in part to the narcissistic energies of the Bolan song, exemplifies the idea, as Hall puts it, that his 'sexual obsession is with himself and his dancing'.[116]

'Children of the Revolution' is used more fragmentedly, the insistent two-note motif of its opening section initiated by Billy's flight away from his father, who has lunged at him at the culmination of a tense confrontation about his involvement in ballet classes. It subsequently accompanies, almost in synchronicity, his angry physical attack on an appropriately named 'Strike Now' poster. The song's conclusion, featuring a scream by Bolan and a final drawn-out chord, reappears at a moment of sexual tension in Debbie's bedroom, their playful pillow fight momentarily turning tender, following a frank discussion of Debbie's parents' marital difficulties and her mother's involvement in dancing as a surrogate for sex – no wonder Billy later asks Mrs Wilkinson directly if she fancies him. Although these

matter-of-fact discussions of 'adult' concerns by pre-pubescent characters – something of a leitmotif of Hall's early dramas about childhood – generated little comment, the frequency of sexually charged swear words in the film raised the question of whether *Billy Elliot* was to be understood as a 'family' or 'adult' film. For their part, Hall and Daldry felt that if the language was toned down, the 'sentimentality is not balanced by something real'.[117] The British Board of Film Classification (BBFC) recognised the potential appeal and relevance of the film to younger children, but were duty-bound to give a film with 'over 50 uses of the word "fuck"' a '15' rating, meaning it could not be viewed by those under that age.[118]

The third T. Rex number, 'I Love to Boogie', plays during Billy's clandestine, one-to-one dance class with Mrs Wilkinson. As with the opening use of 'Cosmic Dancer', Billy cues it up diegetically, having brought in a tape recording as part of a bundle of special items to generate ideas for dancing. But the subsequent routine is too well choreographed to be instantaneous, thus rendering the sequence redolent of a number from a traditional musical, in its stretching of credulity and its emphasis upon wishful escape rather than verisimilitude. The cinematic playfulness is accentuated through some even more audacious cutting between their routine of spins, runs and lifts, and scenes of family members at home: Tony in headphones

bopping while vacuum-cleaning, the grandmother striking ballet poses and the father gargling vaguely in rhythmic and harmonic step with Bolan's vocal. This cross-cutting has a precedent in earlier sequences that juxtapose Billy's dancing classes with scenes of clashes between police and picketers, which can be read symbolically as a differentiation between Billy's creative individuality and the enervating, doomed lockstep of industrial dispute. Here, though, in a way that parallels the pivot of the lyrics between repeated refrains of 'we love ...' and then 'I love to boogie', the implication is that Billy's urges are a commonplace aspect of northern, working-class identity. But this fantasy of a troubled family temporarily transcending their individual problems is punctured by Billy's crestfallen walk back home, the song terminating abruptly to a match cut of him entering his house and shutting the door behind him, darkening the tone appropriately for the next scenes showing Tony and his father having a violent argument about Tony's picketing plans.

Two street dances

The film's characteristic tonal pivoting is also apparent through the differences between its two sequences of Billy dancing through the Everington streets. The first follows another montage cutting back and forth between dance classes and shots of Billy in various locations at home practising and perfecting a double pirouette. Warbeck's unobtrusive score, of tremulous strings and tentative woodwind phrases, momentarily stops to give prominence to Mr Braithwaite's withering 'You look like a right wanker to me, son' put-down, but then returns forcefully with martial brass lines and full orchestral texture to accompany Billy joyfully dancing his way home, his foot movements broadly in synch with flourishes of percussion. For cinematographer Tufano, these dance sequences needed to work 'both as literal action and fantasy',[119] and while the cross-cutting shots of Billy conjuring glissandos and chord clashes on his home piano accentuate the idea of an excited reverie, his swerves and leaps

are captured naturalistically through fluid, responsive camerawork, including some brief dollies using the cinematographer's personalised 'Steadicart' vehicle that marries a Steadicam-type slickness with the 'human feel of lower-budget, edgier film-making'.[120] The choreographer Peter Darling also influenced the decision to ensure kineticism by avoiding longer, static shots in favour of tracking against lamp-posts and other objects in a way to emphasise Billy's speed.

Billy's second street display, triggered by his family members and teacher aggressively squabbling over his potential talent, is commonly labelled his 'angry dance', in reference to a familiar pop-culture trope, perhaps most famously exemplified by Kevin Bacon's expressive routine to a pop song in *Footloose* (1984). Here, The Jam's 'Town Called Malice' (1982), with its soul/mod inflections and lyrics imparting the need to escape spirit-crushing towns (Woking, in the case of singer Paul Weller), makes a sympathetic match for the passionate footwork that pushes Billy up against literal walls, doors, roofs and fences. For Darling, the challenge was to reproduce on film the way that the eye tracks dance movement, even if this went against traditional expectations of focus or editing rhythm. Except for some close-up shots on Billy's tapping feet, the camera initially remains static, with compositions emphasising Billy's hands and feet pushing the edge of the frame.

The moment where Billy runs into his family's outdoor privy, and taps and punches its brick walls, before kicking the door off its hinges to get out, would provide ammunition for those who – missing the blackly humorous play with stereotype – considered the film to be a regressive, unrealistic depiction of working-class experience in the 1980s. The cultural critic Ben Thompson singled out the toilet scene as the exemplar of a type of current film-making that was not so much an antidote to Merchant Ivory-type heritage cinema, but an expansion of their historical gaze to times of 'lurid flock wallpaper and overgrown canal towpaths' via a 'new nostalgia of mud'.[121] A similar idea was articulated more positively by the heritage scholar Andrew Higson, who placed *Billy Elliot* within a strand of films,

also including *Vera Drake* (2004) and *East is East* (1999), noting how 'in their focus on the unheralded and their democratic extension of the range of social types represented on the big screen, they effectively demythologise England and Englishness'.[122]

In the *Guardian*, the journalist and writer John Sutherland queried the contradiction of the film depicting the Elliots as clearly having functional indoor plumbing (evidenced in the bathroom scenes), while still being 'associated with the traditionally primitive sanitation of the British working class' – i.e. the outside toilet.[123] Another question of plausibility that haunts this sequence – which draws some inspiration from the 'mod' moves of Northern Soul dancers, as well as the choreographer and dancer Dein Perry's *Tap Dogs* shows of the 1990s – is the extent to which Billy would have gained this level of tap proficiency from Mrs Wilkinson's ballet classes alone, although we do hear her give a 'now tap!' instruction in the 'I Love to Boogie' number. However, for dance scholar Michael Gard, Billy's athletic, borderline aggressive movements here form part of a strategy to 'reconcile dance and tough, muscular, heterosexual masculinity', and thus position the character as 'anything but queer'.[124] Certainly, Billy's persona here is closer to Gene Kelly's rugged, proletarian athleticism than Fred Astaire's debonair style, and it is also significant that Billy is wearing his father's pit shoes, scuffing and dirtying them in an act of both protest and reclamation.

Billy's ungainly jump from the roof of what seems to be his family coal-shed, causing him to grunt and limp onwards, is followed by compositions showing him either moving away from or towards the camera, as he flees down his back lane, then ascends another street, desperately tapping until he crashes into a corrugated steel fence. In a neat continuity trick, snowfall and the sudden appearance of Billy's overcoat indicate that it is now deep winter, and a time of greater hardship for the striking miners. A few critics singled out the imagery here of Billy running up a steep back lane against the backdrop of a 'cloudless sky over a blue sea on which sails a single, fairy-tale boat heading on some magic journey'.[125] The symbolic

potential is clearly exploited here and elsewhere, such as with the glimpse we get of a sailing-boat decoration in Billy's bedroom once he has shown an interest in ballet classes. The image of a sailing vessel bordered by inclining terraced streets also recalls a history of photography and film-making showing massive ships at the bottom of streets running down to yards, such as on the occasion of a grand launch.[126] Although *Billy Elliot* is of course set elsewhere, in a coastal colliery location that has a *Kes*-like combination of rural and industrial ambience, the replacement of such symbols of proud industry with a faraway pleasure boat carries charges of both defeat and optimism.

London calling

In the film's 'London Calling' sequence, the 1979 song by British rock band The Clash is used to score Tony's flight from and eventual capture by riot police. To describe this as a 'number' may seem like a lapse of taste, but this part of *Billy Elliot* risks the same accusation in the way it presents the chase as a kind of choreographed routine, deploying the synchronisation devices of musical theatre (or music videos) to the recreation of a scarring moment in British political and social history. Fast cutting between long and close shots of riot police driving and assaulting picketers and bystanders (including some Eisenstein-like compositions of strikers being driven diagonally downhill), and those of Tony escaping by running through houses, back lanes and across lawns, generates excitement and suspense. But there is also admiration for his timing, agility and sheer chutzpah, as he springs over a weightlifter, pauses for a moment to take a slurp from an unattended cup of tea and avoids tripping over a space hopper.[127] Like the initial obliviousness of the man calmly washing his car while all hell is breaking loose, these moments have a dark absurdity that matches the cartoon-like aggression of the police and the faintly surreal (and apparently CGI-enhanced) climax, where

Tony finds himself suddenly facing an army of about a hundred of them, all banging their shields in unison, like a warped premonition of the audience coming to see Billy in the film's closing sequence. The sequence also anticipates the defeatist end of the upcoming 'angry dance' number, in the way that Tony's comparably anti-authoritarian flight from and through signifiers of domesticity culminates in him being enveloped, rather suggestively, by white sheets hanging to dry in the alleyways, which turn blood-red as horse-mounted police attack him with truncheons.

The way that the sequence can be read simultaneously as a distressing depiction of the traumatising effect of the miners' strike – as suggested by the scenes of Billy watching powerless as his brother is captured and assaulted – and as a satirically cartoonish take on history has a parallel in the relationship between 'London Calling' and its punk origins. As music scholar Matthew Gelbart argues, the song's parent album of the same name was influential in normalising punk rock – lyrically, sonically, conceptually – for a more mature audience, and thus achieved a 'careful balancing act between punk street-cred and mainstream musical value', a fusion of anti-establishment sentiment and a more universal address.[128] Joe Strummer's lyrical concerns encompass nuclear power, the flooding of the Thames and (most appropriately here) the 'truncheon thing' of police brutality, but also his band's own position within the landscape of commercial music. Musically, 'London Calling' has a hard-rock drive that gives a tough, 'masculine' stab suitable for the depiction of police violence, but also a looser reggae swing more apt for Tony's fleet-footed negotiation of familiar community spaces. The lyrical refrain of 'London Calling' was an explicit reference to the BBC World Service's famous station identification. However, it carries all manner of associative ideas, most directly here the violent incursion into the North East of the forces of the London Metropolitan Police, subtly distinguished in the film from their regional counterparts, but also the clarion call of the capital as the only place Billy can fulfil his creative potential.

In his commentary on deleted scenes included on the DVD release, Stephen Daldry acknowledges that the loss of some material relating to Tony had a simplifying effect on his characterisation as someone who moves a little quickly from hostility to warmth towards his younger brother. The jettisoned scenes include a more nuanced take on the 'scab' character Gary, with whom the Elliot men have an angry confrontation in the supermarket, but later – in the excised material – comes with money to support Billy's cause. The character of neighbour Sheila, only seen briefly in the street, was also originally more fleshed out, gesturing towards the importance of women's support for miners in their community. In Hall's first script, Tony's commitment to the union was emphasised more strongly, including a sequence where he takes Billy to a fundraising concert for the miners in Newcastle, where the Scottish protest singer Dick Gaughan is playing. One of the deleted scenes is a longer version of the Christmas fundraising event glimpsed briefly in the film and includes the boxing instructor George leading a communal rendition of the American unionist song 'Miner's Lifeguard', which is in the repertoire of Gaughan and many other UK folk performers. Changing the focus to the 'ordinary' residents of the village, engaged in a collective rendition of a folk song, this naturalistic sequence involving non-professional actors might have jarred, being more in the spirit of a Ken Loach or Amber film. While the absence of any direct reference to a regional folk music tradition is a pity within the context of the film's more metropolitan (that is, London-centric) pop-music choices, this would be later rectified to some degree within the more musically varied score of the *Billy Elliot* stage musical.

Dances for Dad and Michael

As the last full routine of the film, the so-called 'Dance for Dad' number that Billy performs in the boxing hall is the culmination of his training, a proficient, energetic conglomeration of tapping, kicks, twirls and leaps that persuades his father of his talent needing support. During filming, music from Aaron Copland's 1938 ballet

Billy the Kid was used, but this was replaced with a score by Warbeck that utilises comparable folk-like melodies and rhythms. The musical accompaniment is first heard tinnily in the background when Billy and Michael are larking about, as if being played on a tape recorder, but then appearing more distinctly when the father discovers the scene. The orchestral scoring of the 'Dance for Dad' sequence, like that for the rest of the film, was composed by Stephen Warbeck during post-production, a creative decision that gave the composer, in his words, a 'huge uphill task':

Obviously, those sequences were cut with attention to a kind of musicality, but musical structure wasn't at the forefront of the editor's mind. So, if he wanted to cut from Billy doing a kick, to the face of the dad watching him, for example, that meant that the rhythmic structure was not necessarily what you would choose if you were writing the piece.[129]

Although this meant, for Warbeck, a 'big negotiation with the editor and choreographer', he felt that his score was improved by a better comprehension of the 'emotional journey that the father goes on', resulting in the harmonically and tonally ambiguous passage that accompanies the father's departure from the gym. As Warbeck notes: 'You don't know quite whether he's leaving in anger, or if he's

finally won over to understanding Billy's incredible talent'. Another challenge for Warbeck was how to weave together forms of musical pastiche appropriate to Billy's hybrid movements – which encompass traditional ballet, folk dance, musical theatre and sport-related gestures – without it 'feeling like a magazine, where you turn every page, and the next image is completely unrelated to the previous one'. Part of the solution was to advance the initially spiky and rhythmical lines of melody towards a smoother, more free-flowing theme which 'hopefully joins it together'.[130]

When the same music is used for Billy's audition at the Royal Ballet School, there is greater emphasis upon the bewildered reactions of the panel, and the anxious fidgeting of his waiting father outside the room, than on his actual dance itself. In her 2000 review of the film for *Sight and Sound*, Claire Monk argued that the '15-year ellipsis before the film's rapturous ending leaves much unanswered', including the question of how happily he fitted into ballet school,

'or at what cost'.[131] But there are suggestions about the awkwardness of his transition to a new cultural world in the scenes of Billy and father being overawed by the venue's dignified classical architecture and formal etiquette, of Billy responding violently (and homophobically) to another boy's expression of support, and of the well-meant but patronising 'good luck with the strike' well-wishes of the Principal.

The 'Dance for Dad' in the boxing hall in fact begins as a private performance for Michael, who exhorts him to dance after Billy gives him a ballet lesson, shortly after Michael has made a tentative pass at him. Cynthia Weber has described the ballet instructions given to a tutu-wearing Michael in the boxing ring as constituting the most 'blatantly "queer"' scene in the film.[132] However, this comes between other sequences that arguably

downplay the homoerotic associations of male dance, specifically scenes of Billy brushing off Michael's advances, and of Billy dancing vigorously to reassure his father that his aptitude for ballet should outweigh concerns that he is deviating from traditional gender roles. It is here that Billy delivers a much-quoted line that is usually interpreted as indicative of the film's greater interest in questions of masculinity than of sexuality: 'Just because I like ballet, it doesn't mean I'm a poof, you know.' However, writing in the *Gay Times* in 2001, James Cary Parkes expressed disappointment about the potential messaging for 'young lads watching the movie who are secretly gay':

The sad thing about a really great film like *Billy Elliot* is it spends so much time saying being different doesn't make you a poof that it misses the point that, actually, it does. Being different does make you bent, in all sorts of ways.[133]

For some, the coding of the cross-dressing Michael character as queer – whether in terms of conveying 'fully-blown transvestism'[134] or the signs of being incipiently transgender[135] – was problematic, in the way it potentially 'inoculated' Billy himself against any connotations of homosexuality.[136] In my discussions about *Billy Elliot* with students, colleagues and others, I have encountered a diversity of assessments of the film's 'queerness', and also a desire for me – as author of this book – to reach a decisive verdict on whether the film's handling of Billy's nascent sexuality is inspirational, evasive, nuanced, muddled, contradictory or plain homophobic. While I have heard anecdotally of the film's ongoing and international appeal within the LGBTQ+ community, I am respectful of those who considered the 'gay best friend' trope to be a problematic and over-familiar way to affirm the main character's normative heterosexuality. But I am also appreciative of the film's clear argument that creativity and 'difference' – however defined – are not necessarily signifiers of sexual identity.

(Ride a white) Swan Lake

Billy's final appearance in the story, now aged twenty-five and a solo performer in a London production of *Swan Lake*, is prefigured by an earlier discussion of the ballet's plot with Mrs Wilkinson, as they listen to a cassette tape of the Tchaikovsky score (specifically, from Act II, Scene 10). This happens as they ride across the iconic Transporter Bridge that spans the River Tees at Middlesbrough. There is nothing to justify this journey narratively, given that it would in reality involve Mrs Wilkinson taking a geographical detour of around twenty miles to drive Billy home after a lesson. But it gives another demonstration of Billy soundtracking his own environment and discerning comparable grace between one of the best-known ballet melodies and the movement of the structure's suspended 'gondola' from one bank of the river to the other. It is unclear whether Billy's awestruck gaze upwards is in response to the impressively vertiginous machinery, his choice of music or the effect of their synchronicity, but the film is offering both a slightly cheeky allusion to a regional landmark, and an exemplar of how musicality can be extracted even from the most utilitarian and mechanical objects. This scene also includes Mrs Wilkinson's pithy summary of the *Swan Lake* plot as being about a beautiful woman, forced to be a swan, realising that falling in love with a prince will

'allow her to become a real woman once more'. We can find some explanation for her jaundiced take on the ending – 'he promises to marry her and then goes off with somebody else, of course' – in what we have seen of her own domestic circumstances. However, this warning against happy, fantastical endings is simultaneously a cunning bit of misdirection, nudging us to expect a *Kes*-type resolution to the story, and a warning that the film's upbeat coda may not be all it seems. Mrs Wilkinson's final dismissal of *Swan Lake* as 'only a ghost story' cues up the following sequence, in which – in another of the film's jolting 'needle scratches' – the ballet music abruptly terminates with the grandmother screaming in bed as if haunted by a nightmare. Billy then has a more benign vision of his dead mother in the kitchen, good-naturedly castigating him for drinking milk straight out of the bottle. But to what extent might we also regard the adult Billy as a ghost himself, in the sense of both an unknowable entity, and a symbol of loss to haunt the community and family he leaves behind?

Early scholarly takes on *Billy Elliot*, such as that of Alan Sinfield, tended to interpret the film's feel-good ending, where Billy's father and brother sit in a theatre row with Michael and his (presumed) gay partner, as a utopian vision of social and sexual inclusivity.[137] But such a reading overlooks the ambiguous tone of the final section of the film. The news of Billy's acceptance into ballet school is succeeded by that of the defeat of the unions, and the miners' return to work. There follows a series of melancholic goodbyes with Mrs Wilkinson, Michael, his grandmother, father and brother – and even the raggedy back-lane child identified in the published script as 'snotty little girl'. A recurring visual/editing trope of *Billy Elliot* is that of characters either being 'erased' from the frame or being shown exiting it suggestively. A prominent example is the 'magic trick' where Debbie appears to be 'wiped' by a passing police van. In addition, Michael's final appearance (as a child) is last witnessed in a long shot, disappearing into his house, as if imperceptibly dissolving into his domestic background, while a stoic

Mrs Wilkinson follows her last conversation with Billy by sharply exiting screen left to return to her class. When first seen entering the boxing hall, for his fateful encounter with the ballet class, Billy hovers on the threshold while being hectored by a mooching Michael not to go inside. After the door slam, we stay momentarily with Michael outside, as if Billy has been lost to him and us in some way.

Our last glimpse of Billy as a child is through the windows of the London-bound bus moving blurrily from right to left, following an awkward farewell, in which his father has turned his back to the departing vehicle and he is unable to comprehend the words of his brother – 'I'll miss you' – through the window. Given the recurrence of compositions involving mirrors, reflections and characters framed in screen-like squares and rectangles (such as when Billy's father is first shown watching Billy's boxing lesson), it is also significant that the final images of child Billy are through windows that separate him from his family and put obstacles in the way of mutual comprehension. In this way, in tandem with the equally recurrent imagery of Billy under surveillance by others – his father, Michael, the girls at ballet class, Mrs Wilkinson, the snotty girl, the other professional ballet dancers in the final sequence – we are alerted to how the film frames him, his body and his story, as an object for identification, projection but also, ultimately, mystery.

These closing scenes affected composer Stephen Warbeck, along with the earlier sequence of the father being confronted by Tony when about to cross a picket line. Noting that 'when writing music for films, I try and find a key moment that really affects me emotionally', he was unafraid of the expressive, heightened qualities of the string-driven scoring here:

> The fact that you can't hear the words being spoken, it's almost like you want to create the wave of what's behind those words, without the words being there, like: I love you, I believe in you. The music is there to suggest what the underlying passion or emotion is.[138]

In 'speaking' for the characters and their emotional states, the scoring thus functions here equivalently to the way that songs might do in a standard musical, conveying sentiments that characters struggle to articulate.

Billy Elliot ends with a sequence set around fifteen years later, roughly contemporaneous with the time of the film's release in 2000, showing Billy's father and brother hurriedly making their way through the London underground to the Theatre Royal in Drury Lane, taking their seats just as Billy is advancing his way to the stage for a solo entrance in what the rising musical score tells us is a production of *Swan Lake*. The fragmentary presentation of adult Billy – shot from behind in a white robe flexing his neck like a boxer approaching the ring, and from the side as he bends his head low – generates curtain-raising anticipation when cut to the Tchaikovsky music against his family sitting down next to Michael and his partner. As feel-good and inclusive as this all seems to be, the construction of the sequence only connects Billy and his visiting audience associatively, as they never share the same frame.

The absence in this final sequence of the dance instructor Mrs Wilkinson gives some weight to the charges made of the film's 'effeminophobia'. For Niall Richardson, *Billy Elliot* sits squarely within a social-realist tradition, stretching back to the New Wave films of the late 1950s and early 1960s, of articulating British anxieties about the 'stigma of middle-class effeminacy'.[139] This is a reference to the way that films such as *Saturday Night and Sunday Morning* (1960) emphasised the perspective of young working-class men aggressively resisting the forces of domestic entrapment in the shape of romantic partners with materialistic aspirations. This spirit lives via the character of Billy's brother, who upon discovery of the private dance lessons, threatens violence towards Mrs Wilkinson, describing her as a 'middle-class cow' (and we have indeed seen her home in a more aspirational, tree-lined part of town). It is hard to overlook the limited agency, and eventual invisibility, of the female characters in *Billy Elliot*, even when they are positioned sympathetically as instigators of change and transformation. Mrs Wilkinson leads the process, but Billy's success is also enabled to some degree by a genetic inheritance of creativity from his mother and grandmother, the encouragement of young Debbie, and by the tutor on the audition panel who breaks rank with her inscrutable colleagues to ask him a compassionate question about what it feels like when he is dancing. It is thus a shame that the final part of the film shows the adult Billy performing only to male members of his family, alongside Michael and his partner, and with an exclusively male company.

Significantly, Billy has become the lead in a production of *Swan Lake* that is evidently Matthew Bourne's famously innovative version, first staged in 1995 by his New Adventures company. The costumes and facial make-up, and the playing of adult Billy by the ballet performer Adam Cooper, who created the lead role in Bourne's version, clearly align the film's character with a production widely regarded as one of the most impactful and well-known dance shows of the era. Bourne's production cast men rather than women in the role of the swans, thus introducing elements of homosexual love and desire to the tragic plotting (and alluding to Tchaikovsky's widely assumed homosexuality). But just as relevant as its gender-bending, iconoclastic reputation was its status as a 'crossover'

work of contemporary dance that bridged the traditional with the modern, and – like the *Billy Elliot* musical a decade later – translated successfully to international audiences. We don't get to see much of the actual performance though, other than a powerful balletic soar that dissolves mid-air, to the sound of a sustained, treated orchestral chord, to return us to the opening shots of Billy bouncing in his bedroom. As the credits appear, there is a superimposed image of Adam Cooper performing pirouettes, and then a final return to the young Billy.

For Cynthia Weber, the metatextual allusion to Bourne's production was a sly means of double coding, openly giving a 'wink and a nod to the queer crowd while, for the mainstream audience, dulling the radical edges of queer performances'.[140] But there is a forceful message here about the liberatory potential of physical movement, in offering the potential to trouble or transcend categories of gender, class and sexuality – be it in the form of tap-dancing, boxing, football or even just bopping to Marc Bolan while vacuuming. The final sequence makes an equivalent statement about music too, matching a visual dissolve between past and present with a sonic transition between Tchaikovsky and T. Rex's 'Ride a White Swan' (1970). Not simply a lyrically apposite choice, the song is regarded as a foundation stone of the glam-rock movement. But it also has a primitivism in its instrumentation, riffing, chords and mystical-sounding lyrics, coming together in what music critic Barney Hoskyns describes as an 'electric neo-rockabilly groove'[141] that has a more childlike quality than the sexier, punchier Bolan numbers included elsewhere in the film. As such, this is a return to innocence, encouraging us not to be overwhelmed by the many interpretive and contextual readings that Billy and his story have generated, and to remember the simple pleasures of movement, music and rhythm.[142]

3 Go, Billy! The Legacy of *Billy Elliot*

Debates about *Billy Elliot*'s long-term significance were raging within weeks of its release. In response to an extremely positive review by critic Christopher Tookey – 'a totally home-grown, British-financed triumph'[143] – the critic and writer Gilbert Adair unleashed a critique of the jingoism of UK reviewers inclined to overestimate the durability and reach of British product such as *The English Patient* (1996) and *Shakespeare in Love* (1998). Adair speculated whether *Billy Elliot* – which he judged to be a 'ludicrous luvvie fantasy' – would be a film for the ages.[144] Such misgivings would surely be challenged by this very book's existence and my advocacy for the film's secure place within a canon of creatively significant British cinema.

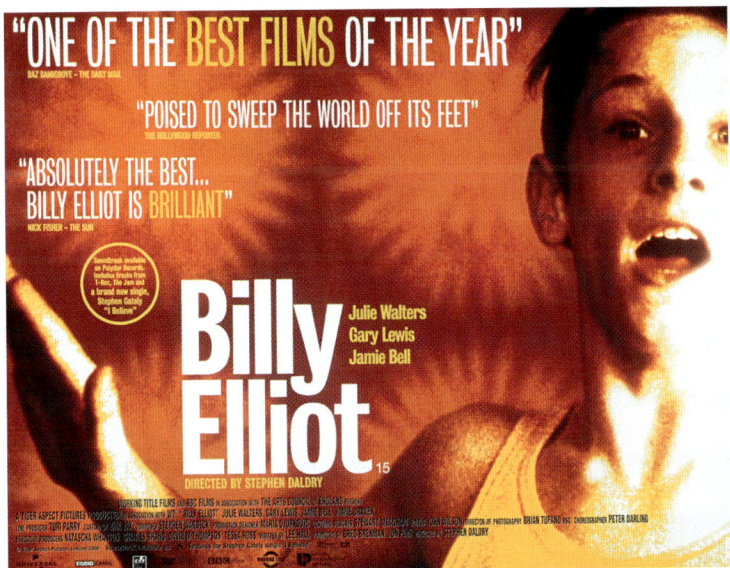

Looking for metrics to demonstrate the impact of *Billy Elliot*, we can point to the box-office takings ($25.2 million in the UK, $109.3 million worldwide),[145] the voluminous journalistic coverage and its many accolades, which included three Oscar nominations, three BAFTA wins (out of twelve nominations) and four successes at the British Independent Film Awards. Just as *Billy Elliot* fused the low and high in its story, style and attitude, so its reach transcended class, politics and sometimes even the bounds of believability. It was no surprise that the film was parodied by television comedians – such as Lenny Henry's quick-off-the-mark 'Billy Idiot' sketch[146] broadcast in December 2000 – and referenced in soap operas such as *EastEnders* (1985–), *Emmerdale* (1972–), *Coronation Street* (1960–) and *Holby City* (1999–2002). Less expected, yet indicative of how Billy had made a vault not just from the North East coalfields to the metropolitan creative industries, but to the upper echelons of society, was the mention of *Billy Elliot* in the Houses of Parliament on the occasions of the death of Margaret Thatcher in April 2013, and of Queen Elizabeth in September 2022. In response to the passing of the former, the Lord Bishop of Oxford conceded that her policies were divisive, and that '"Billy Elliot" country was not an all-singing, all-dancing landscape'.[147] The invocation of the film in the context of a parliamentary eulogy to Thatcher was particularly ironic given that the *Billy Elliot* musical includes a song where the characters raise a toast to the prime minister's future death.[148] And if it was curious to hear, via Baroness Bull's parliamentary remembrance of Queen Elizabeth, that the monarch had made an unofficial visit to see the stage show to 'celebrate her 80th birthday', this at least demonstrated the story's universal appeal.[149]

One of the most beguiling aspects of *Billy Elliot* for many initial viewers and critics was the witnessing in real time of a career launch for its lead actor Jamie Bell. In 2015, he stated that 'unfortunately, my entire life was basically made by *Billy Elliot*. It was kind of created by that one catalytic moment.'[150] However, his professional career has proved to be of a very different order to that of his spiritual forebear

Jamie Bell (Dave Hogan/MP/Getty Images)

David (Dai) Bradley, who came to be, as David Forrest observes in his BFI Film Classic book on the film, 'entirely defined' by his teenage role in *Kes*.[151] In some respects, the comparison is unfair, as Bell was already a more experienced performer, even appearing in the lead role in a stage production of *Kes* a short time before *Billy Elliot* was released.[152] Still, it took a while for reviewers to identify him as having shaken off the associations of his debut film, such as with film critic Philip Kemp's assessment that his performance in *Hallam Foe* (2007) 'lastingly lays the ghost of cute Billy Elliot'.[153] Yet, Bell's film work to date – encompassing some bigger-budget Hollywood projects like *The Adventures of Tintin* (2011) but also edgier British fare such as *Filth* (2013) and roles for international auteurs such as Lars von Trier and Bong Joon Ho – is in the spirit of *Billy Elliot*'s challenge to straightforward generic and national codification, and its character's intuitive rejection of artistic compartmentalisation. He also undertook an intriguingly metatextual exorcism of the character when playing a spectral mid-1980s father in Andrew Haigh's *All of Us Strangers* (2023), a role he understood as a 'kind of bookend' to that of Billy Elliot, reversing the polarities of the original film so as to play, in the words of the director, a 'father to a son who's struggling, rather than a boy who's struggling with his dad'.[154]

Bell's story had a darker counterpart in the decision made by Stuart Wells, who played Billy's friend Michael, to abandon acting in 2001 for a military career. Turning eighteen at the time of the film's release, he told reporters of his sense of fraudulence as an actor – having been originally approached by a talent scout at a skateboarding park – but also that his role had embarrassed him. In an uncomfortable variation on the film's critique of gendered attitudes, he disowned the film in a 2001 interview for the *Daily Mail*, criticising Daldry for editing material to leave him 'looking like a sissy' and expressing optimism that an army career would make a 'man' of him.[155]

Billy Elliot was no less transformative for the members of its core creative team – of director Stephen Daldry, writer Lee Hall, producer Jon Finn and choreographer Peter Darling – who adapted the film into a musical, scored by Elton John, that ran in London's West End between 2005 and 2016, and in various worldwide incarnations. Furthermore, in 2014, a live cinema relay of the show topped the weekend box-office chart in the UK, the first time that a 'piece of alternative content' had done so.[156] With a longer running time affording the reinstatement of elements that had fallen away from the film on its progression from initial draft to final cut, the musical gave more attention to the attitudes and conflicts of those involved in strike activity. It also used a broader palette of musical styles – from hymnal choruses, music hall, pantomime and traditional Broadway-type numbers to pop pastiche and regional folk song – to complement its equivalent diversity of dance movements, and to convey the rich variety of working-class culture. For theatre scholar Robert Gordon, one of the musical's key achievements was to be 'the first mainstream British entertainment to directly interrogate homophobic prejudice as a function of patriarchal society'.[157] This can be seen most explicitly in the way that the staging and choreography 'queers' the hyper-masculinity of the miners, in numbers such as the complexly choreographed 'Solidarity', which has policemen and striking miners singing threats at each other as their respective headgear get muddled, and their movements become integrated with those of the ballet class rehearsing their routine. The musical also strikes a balance between meeting and frustrating the expectations of those familiar with the movie. Some moments in the original that felt like musical numbers in waiting, such as Billy's speech about how dancing feels like 'electricity', are duly transformed into song lyrics. But there is no place for Marc Bolan, or bed-bouncing, and the 'dream ballet' of a young and adult Billy dancing together – the equivalent of the film's concluding time-leap – occurs earlier, resulting in a more overtly downbeat ending emphasising the defeat of the miners and the plight of those left behind in Easington.

If the musical was more elegiac than the original source, this was in part a reflection of Hall's newfound realisation, in the years between writing the film and its stage successor, that *Billy Elliot* was fundamentally a lament for heavy industry and the communities and lives around it.

What I didn't realise at the time is that I was writing a much bigger story than the kid dancing, or what happened to the pits: the deindustrialisation of Britain, and the end of that formulation of the working class. It was less obvious living through it than it was later, even though I was predicting it and wanted to write about it. I remember going around the coalfields with my dad to think about locations and being shocked that the pit heads had been levelled – a cultural cleansing going on already in the mid-1990s, ten years after the strike. By the time we made the movie there were hardly any pits left at all.[158]

Although Hall is, by any criterion, a successful writer for film, television and theatre, his career in cinema, almost exclusively as an adaptor of books, plays or biographical material, has not followed the smooth curve of *Billy Elliot*'s leap to prominence – with abandoned works, compromised outcomes and detachments from projects completed by others. His most critically feted work to date has arguably been his stage play *The Pitmen Painters*, a true story based on William Feaver's book of the same name, about a group of Ashington miners in the 1930s who wanted to study art appreciation via the Workers Education Association but were persuaded by their tutor Robert Lyon to take up painting themselves, eventually having their work collected and admired by the British art establishment. First performed at the Live Theatre in Newcastle in 2007, *The Pitmen Painters* can be understood as a loose prequel to *Billy Elliot*, in its thesis about the transformative possibility of art for all, and exemplification of how 'culture is for living, not commodification, and art should be about taking part'.[159] The play also tacitly addresses the critique of *Billy Elliot* as being a justification for the aspiring artist having no choice but to escape their provincial, working-class environment for a place of greater resource. The play considers the dilemma of Oliver Kilbourn, one of the younger coalfield painters, who refuses the opportunity of paid patronage by an art collector – but unlike Billy, he chooses to remain within his community.

If *Billy Elliot*'s impact on British theatre was unmistakable, its effect on British film-making of the twenty-first century has been more diffuse than direct. Just as *Billy Elliot* had been trailed in the trade and popular press as the 'next *Full Monty*', so the hunt was on to identify the next *Billy Elliot*. One of the most likely candidates was Gurinder Chadha's *Bend It Like Beckham* (2002), which similarly told an inspirational culture-clash story through a combination of humour and pathos. However, from a distance we can now identify this populist, fable-like approach to working-class experience as very much of its time. Hall says that he has since tried to reproduce these qualities in later screenplays, but 'people don't want that form anymore'.[160] A disdainful attitude to *Billy Elliot* can certainly be observed by reviewers using its perceived shortcomings to spotlight the achievements of other social-realist film-makers occupying similar thematic terrain. Take, for example, film critic Peter Matthews's description of director Ken Loach and writer Paul Laverty, in films such as *Sweet Sixteen*, as telling stories about 'protagonists whose experiences are typical – not one-off overachievers to feed the audience's syrupy fantasies': a clear dig at the *Billy Elliot* phenomenon.[161]

But if the precise *Billy Elliot* formula never quite took flight, its playful, subversive approach to one of the UK's most recognisable forms of indigenous cinematic storytelling would continue to resonate in films as varied as hip-hop musical *1 Day* (2009) and the 'realist horror' *Eden Lake* (2008). *Billy Elliot* was also an early bellwether indicator of a tendency in British film towards what film scholar Louis Bayman has defined as 'retro-heritage'. This refers to a type of cinema that shares the concern of earlier 'heritage' films based on literary texts – most emblematically, Merchant Ivory productions such as *A Room with a View* (James Ivory, 1985) – with 'the eclipse of a certain class-based lifestyle by something recognisably newer'. But this 'retro' version is distinguished from previous heritage production by its popular, feel-good quality, and focus on the working and lower middle classes of the more recent past.[162] Hall's 'fantasy' autobiography, with its occasionally playful use of period decor and props, was an early example of a notably long-running and important cycle of very personal 'rites of passage' takes on the 1980s by auteurs such as Shane Meadows and Joanna Hogg. These have been supplemented by other films like *Blinded by the Light* (2019) and *Censor* (2021), which have found contemporary resonances in the decade's less enlightened politics of identity. *Billy Elliot* also typified the new route of heritage adaption as from film to stage musical, rather than from novel or stage play to film, anticipating the way that the likes of *Made in Dagenham* (2010) and *Pride* (2014) would be translated for the theatre.

Although its prominent use of 'retro' pop music on the soundtrack was a well-established trope of 1990s British cinema – a characteristic shared by youth/cult films such as *Trainspotting* (1996) as well as the Richard Curtis rom-com cycle – *Billy Elliot*'s musical selections had (more or less) a coherence and conceptual significance that anticipated the rise of one of the most successful genres of twenty-first-century British film-making. Examples of the 'jukebox' musical, either of biographical inspiration or exploiting the output of a particular artist, include *Mamma Mia* (2008) and *Bohemian*

Rhapsody (2018). The Hall-scripted *Rocketman* (2019), based on Elton John's rise to pop stardom, could even be regarded as vaguely in the *Billy Elliot* universe, given the parallels that the singer has identified between his own family background and that of the Elliot family,[163] his scoring of the *Billy Elliot* musical and the casting of Jamie Bell in the film in the role of his writing partner Bernie Taupin.

When Hall first conceived of *Billy Elliot*, barely a decade had passed since the end of the miners' strike in 1985, and aside from its coverage in Peter Flannery's historical epic *Our Friends in the North*, the topic had barely been broached directly in popular British screen culture – although in Billy's native North East, the Amber photographic and film collective were rigorously documenting the impact of de-industrialisation of the Durham coalfields in their trilogy of *The Scar* (1997), *Like Father* (2001) and *Shooting Magpies* (2005).[164] In her examination of recent cultural representations of the strike, Katy Shaw observes how it stereotypically functions as a 'backdrop to the personal stories which audiences are asked to prioritise over and above the cause, nature and function of the collective'.[165] Indeed, one of the oft-heard criticisms of *Billy Elliot* is that its use of the strike as a narrative frame for Billy's evolution as a dancer gives limited scope for an explanation of the causes of the dispute, its effect upon communities like Easington, or the practical and campaigning roles that women played to support the miners (although, as noted above, some material relating to these ideas was cut from the finished film along the way).

However, a more sympathetic take is that *Billy Elliot* helped to lift the burden of representation accrued by the miners' strike and its legacy, allowing film and television makers to approach the subject from a multiplicity of aesthetic, thematic and political perspectives – from Mike Figgis's documentation (2001) of conceptual artist Jeremy Deller's re-enactment of the Battle of Orgreave, and Bill Morrison's poetic collage *The Miners' Hymns* (2010), to the crime series *Sherwood* (2022–). *Billy Elliot*'s tonal influence was felt most clearly in the similarly emotive and uplifting *Pride*, based on the true story of a support group established by a London lesbian and gay activist organisation for a mining community in South Wales. If *Billy Elliot* was a musical trying to escape from a Ken Loach project, *Pride* ran with themes about queer identity and activism that were barely latent or subtextual in *Billy Elliot*. As Niall Richardson observes, *Billy Elliot* has a kinship with *Pride* in the way that their narratives are interrupted through instances of song, music or dancing that also provide a 'meta-critical commentary on the film's themes'.[166] If Billy's dance for his father functions as a commentary on the anger of the miners, so the musical interludes in *Pride* situate the strike within the context of activist history. Additionally, *Pride* boldly flips the direction of spectatorship, telling its story of alliance through the perspective of LGBTQ+ characters who direct their gaze and interest onto the predominantly heteronormative world of the mining community. This contrasts with the way the secondary character of Michael in *Billy Elliot* is configured as a misfit in Everington, narratively othered through his near-obsessive sexual interest in Billy. Jon Finn, the producer who oversaw the film and theatrical versions of *Billy Elliot*, has emphasised how the intervening years have exposed the prescience of their handling of Michael's sexuality.[167] While the film-makers had been under pressure from some quarters to remove the scenes involving the Michael/Billy kisses, and there were reports of early audiences at the stage show responding negatively to these too, by the end of the musical's run these moments were customarily met by standing ovations.

    As for Ken Loach, whose *Kes* had always been the 'lodestar of ambition' for the creators of *Billy Elliot*,[168] the choice of a Durham former-coalfield setting for the film widely publicised as his final work, *The Old Oak* (2023), underscored how the region's deprivation was now a recognised symbol of the devastating social and economic effects of de-industrialisation. Loach's film concerns a pub landlord whose support for Syrian refugees stirs traumatic recollections of the miners' strike and its aftermath, and features a scene where the two main characters visit Durham Cathedral, a site with deeply symbolic resonance in the region's industrial history, as the venue for the service that traditionally marks the culmination of the annual Durham Miners' Gala. Given that this is the cathedral that young Billy Elliot claims never to have visited (when asked about it by a boy at the ballet school audition), we are invited to consider

The Old Oak (2023)

The Old Oak, which also concludes with footage of the Gala banner procession in Durham city centre, as a re-politicising of the environment of the earlier film – or to formulate it in familiar terms, to applaud a Loach film commanding its way back to *Billy Elliot* country.[169]

Beyond its impact on British film-making, *Billy Elliot* has been widely cited as an inspiration for young dancers, particularly boys or those from less privileged backgrounds. Within months of the film's release, newspapers dispatched journalists to dance classes and schools across the country, who came back with assessments about how 'dance has become democratised in Britain'.[170] Speaking in 2002, the Royal Ballet-schooled Adam Cooper, who played the older Billy in the film, stated that 'people now realise that ballet dancing is in fact a very physical, athletic, manly job to do'.[171] The passing of time would result in some more nuanced reflections that either judged the film's impact to be a myth,[172] an overstatement[173] or to be at the expense of nurturing female ballet students.[174] However, the 'Billy Elliot effect' was also cited in discussions about arts funding or educational schemes for under-privileged children, and would occasionally be interpreted not in connection with Billy's creative achievements, but in relation to the attitudes initially expressed by his father. In January 2022, a 'Case for Culture' report by the Northern Culture All-Party Parliamentary Group of MPs, cultural leaders and metropolitan mayors highlighted a persistent attitude whereby 'creative careers are regarded as a form of failure or a waste of education and potential', and thus a barrier to access to working-class youngsters in communities, such as those in Easington, utterly changed by de-industrialisation.[175]

If *Billy Elliot* retained its relevance as a cultural touchstone through the eras of New Labour, Coalition and Conservative rule – an aspirational narrative of transformation that resonated equally with successive political philosophies of Blairism, austerity, Brexit completion and 'levelling up' – it was also deemed by some to anticipate one of the key trends in popular television entertainment of the twenty-first century. For critic Nick James, *Billy Elliot* 'foreshadowed the Blairite world of reality-TV talent shows such as *The X Factor*',[176] its release coinciding with the rise of the international *Popstars* and *Idols* franchises, interactive competitive shows that launched successful pop careers. These in turn inspired musical-theatre and dancing variations, most famously *Strictly Come Dancing* (2004–), which had an equivalent reputational effect in the dancing world to *Billy Elliot*. However, as far-sighted as *Billy Elliot* apparently was in forecasting the Cinderella narratives and emotionally weaponised 'sob stories' of *X Factor*-type reality shows, it was a film – and later musical – already rooted in a tradition of participatory, demotic entertainment, whether popular forms of regional theatre, or the long-standing yet disappearing tradition of 'go as you please' talent competitions in many working-class towns and villages across the UK.

Billy Elliot is a film rooted in all kinds of industrial, popular and cultural traditions, and a lament for what has been lost or forgotten. In time, we have come to understand it better as both a coda for the 1980s and 1990s – for the legacy of the miners' strike and the impact of de-industrialisation – and as the curtain-raising overture for the twenty-first-century world of reality TV, political tribalism and high-performance cultures. But then we remember its eponymous character, with his one foot on the ground, the other in mid-air, soaring between the past and the future, between then and now. Billy inspires us to find the music wherever we are.

Notes

1 John Hill, 'A Working-Class Hero is Something to Be?', in Phil Powrie, Ann Davies and Bruce Babington (eds), *The Trouble with Men: Masculinities in American and European Cinema* (London: Wallflower Press, 2004), pp. 100–9.
2 Paul Marris, 'Northern Realism: An Exhausted Tradition?', *Cineaste* 26, no. 4 (2001), pp. 47–50, p. 48.
3 Michael Wayne, 'Working Title Mark II: A Critique of the Atlanticist Paradigm for British Cinema', *International Journal of Media & Cultural Politics* 2, no. 1 (2006), pp. 59–73.
4 For example, in an interview for the *Here's the Thing* podcast in December 2011, Daldry said: 'I think the stage show is better than the movie; it found its natural home'. Available at: <https://www.wnycstudios.org/podcasts/heresthething/episodes/176487-stephen-daldry?tab=transcript> (accessed 4 June 2024).
5 Dominic Sandbrook, *The Great British Dream Factory: The Strange History of Our National Imagination* (London: Allen Lane, 2015), p. 1040 (e-pub).
6 Neil Archer, *Cinema and Brexit: The Politics of Popular English Film* (London and New York: Bloomsbury, 2021), p. 231.
7 This would become the first of a quartet of interconnected radio plays – eventually known as the 'God's Country' cycle – that explored notions of death and faith from a child's perspective. The concluding play, *Spoonface Steinberg* (1997), a monologue by an autistic girl dying of cancer, became an immediate talking point, famously causing teary lorry drivers to pull off motorways when it was broadcast on BBC Radio 4.

8 Hall interviewed in Alistair Owen, *Story and Character: Interviews with British Screenwriters* (London: Bloomsbury, 2016), p. 40.
9 Lee Hall, *Plays: 1* (London: Methuen, 2002), p. xii.
10 Lee Hall, interview with author, 27 February 2024.
11 Lee Hall, *Billy Elliot* (London: Faber and Faber, 2000), p. viii.
12 Ibid.
13 Martin Hunt, 'The Poetry of the Ordinary: Terence Davies and the Social Art Film', *Screen* 40, no. 1 (Spring 1999), pp. 1–16.
14 Curiously, one of Barry Hines's early screenplay drafts contained a scene where a visiting theatre company called 'Opera for All' perform to a nonplussed, bored audience at Billy's school, thus prophesying but also gently satirising the kind of culture-clash conceit behind *Billy Elliot*. Anon., 'Kes Typescript', Barry Hines Papers, University of Sheffield, KES 3/1, p. 65.
15 Hall, *Billy Elliot*, p. ix.
16 Hall in Owen, *Story and Character*, p. 42.
17 Ibid., p. 49.
18 See, for example, Aleks Sierz, *In-Yer-Face Theatre: British Drama Today* (London: Faber and Faber, 2014).
19 Dominic Dromgoole, *The Full Room: The A–Z of Contemporary Playwriting* (London: Methuen, 2000), p. 121.
20 Hall's preoccupation with childhood also had a correlation with the disturbing imagery found in the work of some of the so-called Young British Artists, such as that by the Chapman Brothers and Marcus Harvey, and also

in the 'dark' television comedy of the era – for example, the controversial 2001 episode of Chris Morris's *Brass Eye* series (1997–2001) satirising the media reporting of paedophilic crimes.

21 Tony Blair first set this out in his address to the Labour Party Conference in Blackpool on 1 October 1996.

22 Hall, interview with author.

23 Hilary Whitney, 'theartsdesk Q&A: Dramatist Lee Hall', *The Arts Desk* (2 October 2011). Available at: <https://www.theartsdesk.com/theatre/theartsdesk-qa-dramatist-lee-hall> (accessed 3 July 2024).

24 Hall, interview with author.

25 For an account of Live Theatre's history and broader position within the theatre culture of North East England, see Andrew John Latimer, 'Beyond "Geordierama": Theatre and Performance in North East England, 2017–18', PhD thesis, Newcastle University (July 2022), pp. 24–58; Natasha Vall, *Cultural Region: North East England 1945–2000* (Manchester and New York: Manchester University Press, 2011), pp. 84–90.

26 Hall, *Plays: 1*, p. ix. For his A-level drama course Hall wrote an essay considering how various productions in Newcastle had been influenced by playwright and drama theorist John McGrath's conceptualisation of a politicised (that is, socialist) working-class theatre, distinct from bourgeois traditions, through elements of 'directness, comedy, music, emotion, variety, effect, immediacy and localism'. John McGrath was a writer for film, television and theatre, and founder of the agitprop 7:84 Theatre Company. Maria DiCenzo, 'John McGrath and Popular Political Theatre', in Mary Luckhurst (ed.), *A Companion to Modern British and Irish Drama 1880–2005* (Oxford: Blackwell, 2006), pp. 419–28, p. 424.

27 Hall, interview with author.

28 For an overview of Amber's film production, see James Leggott, *In Fading Light: The Films of the Amber Collective* (New York and Oxford: Berghahn, 2020).

29 With this reference to the 'backyard', Hall is partly invoking a writing philosophy shared among Live Theatre writers, including Alan Plater, whose autobiographical play *Tales from the Backyard* was performed at the venue in 2001.

30 Ibid.

31 Ibid.

32 Lee Hall, 'Elton John has been taken from the theatre on a stretcher – it's a hit', *Guardian* (4 May 2005). Available at: <https://www.theguardian.com/stage/2005/may/04/dance.westend> (accessed 2 July 2024).

33 Jenny Gilbert, 'From Pit to Point isn't such a far-fetched leap', *Independent* (24 September 2000), p. 7.

34 Rob McGibbon, 'I've been training to become a Samurai sword fighter for months', *Daily Mail* (8 July 2016). Available at: <https://www.dailymail.co.uk/femail/article-3681128/The-definite-article-ask-celebrity-set-devilishly-probing-questions-accept-definitive-answer-week-s-dancer-choreographer-Wayne-Sleep.html> (accessed 4 July 2024).

35 Richard Morrison, 'Did I inspire Billy Elliot? Yes, but it's not on my CV', *The Times* (3 June 2024), p. 9.
36 Anne Woods, 'A Critical Survey of BBC Films 1988–2013', PhD thesis, University of Portsmouth (January 2015), p. 154.
37 The BBC's premiere screening of *Billy Elliot* on New Year's Day 2003 was reported to have 12.7 million viewers, making it the most-watched film broadcast of that year (and in overall ninth place for all broadcasts). Ju-Lin Tan, 'Tricky Dicky Helps Corrie Win Ratings Battle', *Press Association* (7 January 2004).
38 Woods, 'A Critical Survey', p. 155.
39 Ibid.
40 Greg Brenman, interview with author, 12 March 2024.
41 Adam Dawtrey, 'More comedies on plate of Tiger Aspect pic slate', *Variety* (24 November 1997), p. 28.
42 Roanna Benn, interview with author, 27 November 2024.
43 Hall, interview with author.
44 Brenman, interview with author.
45 Jon Finn, interview with author, 6 March 2024.
46 Ibid.
47 Geoffrey Macnab, *Stairways to Heaven: Rebuilding the British Film Industry* (London and New York: I. B. Tauris, 2018), p. 290 (e-pub).
48 Adam Minns, 'Spotlight: Can Low-cost WT² Stay Sweet?', *Screen International* 1265 (30 June 2000), p. 24.
49 Adam Dawtrey, 'Heavyweight helmers head to Working Title', *Variety* (9 December 2000), p. 8.
50 Nathan Townsend, 'WT²: A Low Budget Experiment in "Heart, Humour and Horror"', *Studies in European Cinema* 16, no. 1 (2019), pp. 38–54, p. 39.
51 Ibid., p. 52.
52 Finn, interview with author.
53 York Membery, 'Watch Out Sam, here's Stephen', *Evening Standard* (27 July 2000), p. 35.
54 Woods, 'A Critical Survey', p. 154.
55 Nick James, 'A Matter of Tone', *Sight and Sound* 17, no. 8 (August 2007), p. 5.
56 Adam Dawtrey, 'Brit pic biz bullish now that "Billy"'s a dilly', *Variety* (9 October 2000), pp. 4, 61, p. 4.
57 Of Working Title's acceptance of plaudits, he said: 'they're very big boys and big boys tend to be louder than little boys, but Bevan and Fellner are extremely selective about their projects, and then they give them their full support'. Carla Power, 'The Hitmakers', *Newsweek* (16 October 2000), p. 66.
58 Dawtrey, 'Brit pic biz bullish', p. 61.
59 It also anticipated some of Daldry's later films, which often involve young characters and/or stories of loss taking place against the backdrop of traumatic biographical or historical events: for instance, the Holocaust in *The Reader* (2008) and the 11 September attacks in *Extremely Loud & Incredibly Close* (2011).
60 Edward Lawrenson, 'Cosmic Dancer', *Sight and Sound* 10, no. 10 (October 2000), pp. 12–13, p. 12.
61 Saul Metzstein, 'Grit and Polish', *Sight and Sound* 11, no. 5 (2001), pp. 12–13, p. 12.
62 Ibid., p. 12.

63 Lawrenson, 'Cosmic Dancer', p. 12.
64 Hall, *Billy Elliot*, p. ix.
65 Given that *Educating Rita* was one of her defining roles, there was some piquancy to Walters now playing the teacher in a Pygmalion-esque scenario of transformation.
66 Heather Neill, 'Interview: Jamie Bell', *The Times Educational Supplement* (15 September 2000), p. 21.
67 Daldry speaking in the 2007 episode on the film in the BBC series *Movie Connections* (2007–9).
68 The irony of the Arts Council formally transferring its film-funding power to the Film Council within a few weeks of *Billy Elliot* becoming a commercial success was not lost on contemporary commentators, who identified the film as one of the only recipients of the much-criticised Lottery funding scheme of the last four years to pay back its grant. Anon., 'Editorial: muck, brass and movies', *The Times* (28 September 2000), p. 23.
69 James Caterer, '"Carrying a Cultural Burden": British Film Policy and its Products', *Journal of British Cinema and Television* 5, no. 1 (May 2008), pp. 146–56, p. 154.
70 Ibid., p. 153.
71 Peter Darling, interview with author, 1 May 2024.
72 Ibid.
73 Alice Fowler, 'Inside story', *Mail on Sunday* (23 July 2000), Night and Day, pp. 6–10, p. 7.
74 Neill, 'Interview: Jamie Bell', p. 21.
75 William Russell, 'Attention paid to miner characters', *The Herald* (1 August 2000), p. 17.
76 *Billy Elliot* press notes, *Billy Elliot* clippings file, accessed in BFI Reuben Library.
77 Darling, interview with author.
78 Hall, 'Elton John has been taken from the theatre on a stretcher'.
79 David Jones, 'The real world of Billy Elliot', *Daily Mail* (30 September 2000), pp. 28–9, p. 28.
80 Hall, 'Elton John has been taken from the theatre on a stretcher'.
81 Maureen Taylor-Gooby, *The Birth of Billy Elliot Land: The Beginnings of Easington, Horden and Blackhall Collieries* (Cambridge: Searching Finance, 2015), p. 221.
82 Article by Tony Kearney in the *Northern Echo* (4 March 2009) cited in ibid., p. 222.
83 Finn, interview with author.
84 Robert Chalmers, 'Shaft: the movie', *Independent* (19 May 2000), Review, pp. 1, 7, p. 1.
85 Brenman, interview with author.
86 Michael K. Bosley, '*Billy Elliot*: A Triumphant Grand Jeté', *American Cinematographer* 81, no. 12 (2000), pp. 16–18, p. 16.
87 There is evidence of some late-stage post-dubbing in some dialogue discrepancies between the published script and the film as released; for example, there are differences in the long-shot conversations between Billy and his grandmother when visiting the graveyard, and between Billy and Michael when they are cross-country running.
88 Finn, interview with author.
89 Allan Hunter, 'Dancer', *Screen International* 1261 (2 June 2000), p. 20.

90 Hall, 'Elton John has been taken from the theatre on a stretcher'. This did not literally happen to the singer, but by all accounts, he was emotionally overcome.
91 This is according to Jon Finn, interview with author. The actor Julie Walters corroborates the idea of the parent company as saviour in her autobiography, saying 'things were looking grim until two people from Universal came to a screening and said "We like it"'. Julie Walters, *That's Another Story* (London: Weidenfeld & Nicolson, 2008), p. 244.
92 Ellen Baskin, 'For Universal, it's a new dance', *Los Angeles Times* (8 October 2008), p. G22.
93 Press Release, 'Stephen Daldry's Dancer Changes Title to *Billy Elliot*', Billy Elliot clippings file, accessed in BFI Reuben Library.
94 Of course, as a surrogate of sorts for the burgeoning writer, the Billy character has a name that happens to be an expansion of Lee Hall's first name, just as the Billy character in *Kes* is a near-homophone of the first name of the writer Barry Hines.
95 Finn, interview with author.
96 David Forrest, *Kes* (London: BFI/Bloomsbury, 2024), p. 43.
97 Darling, interview with author.
98 Limor Roichman, 'Dance on Screen', PhD thesis, Middlesex University (2001), p. 95.
99 Hall in Owen, *Story and Character*, p. 49.
100 Hall, interview with author. In a 1971 interview to promote *Electric Warrior*, Bolan clarified his identification with the Cosmic Dancer who, as the lyrics convey, 'dances his way out of the womb and into the tomb', but also declared that he was 'serious about the music but I'm not serious about the fantasy' – a provocation echoed in a statement Hall made in 2002 about how his radio play *Children of the Rain* (2000) exemplified his dramatic strategy in trying to 'have its cake and eat it, to take the piss but also keep the seriousness of the message'. Hall, *Plays: 1*, p. xiii.
101 Hall's planned use of Bolan songs to soundtrack *Billy Elliot* was in keeping with some of his other dramas of the time: for instance, the use of Maria Callas arias in *Spoonface Steinberg*, the composer Handel in *I Luv U Jimmy Spud* and Elvis Presley in *Cooking with Elvis*.
102 Hall, interview with author.
103 Philip Auslander, *Performing Glam Rock: Gender and Theatricality in Popular Music* (Ann Arbor: University of Michigan Press, 2006), p. 6.
104 Billy's story has parallels with Clark, a farmer's son from near Aberdeen who won a place at the Royal Ballet School in 1975, but Clark's career over the next twenty years was more nonconformist and idiosyncratic than what is suggested of Billy, who we see taking the relatively traditional role of lead dancer with a large company in a central London theatre.
105 Hall, interview with author. 'Cosmic Dancer' was also the name of an exhibition retrospective of Clark's career, first shown at the Barbican Centre in 2020.
106 Bob Stanley, *Yeah Yeah Yeah: The Story of Modern Pop* (London: Faber and Faber, 2013), p. 240.

107 Stephen Warbeck, interview with author, 14 October 2024.
108 Ibid.
109 Dyer's article was first published in *Movie* journal (1977). Richard Dyer, 'Entertainment and Utopia', in Dyer (ed.), *Only Entertainment*, 2nd edn (London: Routledge, 2002), pp. 19–35, p. 20.
110 The boxing-hall scenes have a tenuous link to one of cinema's most gifted physical performers, as they were filmed in Hanwell Community Centre in London, formerly part of the Victorian poor school where Charlie Chaplin was homed for a time. The cinematographer describes the film crew discovering a plaque on the walls that indicated Chaplin had been resident. Bosley, 'Billy Elliot', p. 18.
111 Ibid., p. 16.
112 Cynthia Weber, '"Oi, Dancing Boy!" Masculinity, Sexuality, and Youth in *Billy Elliot*', *Genders* 37 (15 January 2003). Available at: <https://www.colorado.edu/gendersarchive1998-2013/2003/01/15/oi-dancing-boy-masculinity-sexuality-and-youth-billy-elliot> (accessed 1 May 2024).
113 Ibid.
114 This was filmed in the Lynemouth area of Northumberland; the Alcan Lynemouth Aluminium Smelter, opened in 1974, ceased production in 2012 and was demolished in 2018.
115 Tony Harrison, *Selected Poems*, 2nd edn (London: Penguin, 1987), p. 238.
116 Lee Hall, 'Script Comments: An Interview with Lee Hall', *Creative Screenwriting* 8, no. 1 (January/February 2001), pp. 14–15, p. 15.
117 Ibid.
118 BBFC, *BBFC Annual Report* (2000), p. 6. The BBFC correspondence files on the film include letters from the public, some decrying the '15' rating on the grounds of bad language as harsh, but others believing it to have gratuitous swearing and problematic representation of pre-adolescent sexual exploration. The BBFC rating generated some press coverage, and also the decision by borough councillors in Tewkesbury to lower it to '12'. There would be similar controversies with two other British realist films being rated higher than the age of their child protagonists, Ken Loach's *Sweet Sixteen* and Shane Meadows's *This Is England* (2006). See Anon., 'Censors defend rating for hit movie', *Gloucestershire Echo*, (1 December 2000), p. 268.
119 Metzstein, 'Grit and Polish', p. 13.
120 Ibid.
121 Ben Thompson, 'Time to give Billy Elliot the boot', *Independent* (5 January 2001), p. 11.
122 Andrew Higson, *Film England: Culturally English Filmmaking Since the 1990s* (London and New York: I. B. Tauris, 2011), p. 244.
123 John Sutherland, 'On outside bogs: the call of the wild', *Guardian* (13 November 2000), p. 7.
124 Michael Gard, *Men Who Dance: Aesthetics, Athletics & the Art of Masculinity* (New York: Peter Lang, 2006), p. 202.
125 Phillip French, 'Film of the Week: the great leap forward', *Observer* (1 October 2000), Review, p. 6.
126 One example can be found in the final sequence of the Amber film

Launch (1974), depicting the send-off of a large ship constructed at the Swan Hunter shipyard in Wallsend.

127 A rubber ball with a face and handles for a child to ride/bounce, the toy known in the UK as the space hopper is – like the Rubik's Cube and KerPlunk game placed noticeably in Billy's bedroom – a comedically overfamiliar signifier of 1970s/1980s childhood.

128 Matthew Gelbart, 'A Cohesive Shambles: The Clash's "London Calling" and the Normalization of Punk', *Music & Letters* 92, no. 2 (May 2011), pp. 230–72, p. 272.

129 Warbeck, interview with author.

130 Ibid.

131 Claire Monk, 'Billy Elliot', *Sight and Sound* 10, no. 10 (October 2000), p. 40.

132 Weber, '"Oi, Dancing Boy!"'.

133 James Cary Parkes, 'Darling's Boy', *Gay Times* (January 2001), pp. 21–2, p. 21.

134 Alan Sinfield, 'Boys, Class and Gender: From Billy Casper to Billy Elliot', *History Workshop Journal* no. 62 (2006), pp. 166–71, p. 166.

135 Niall Richardson, 'Gender, Sexuality and British Cinema', in John Hill (ed.), *A Companion to British and Irish Cinema* (Hoboken, NJ: John Wiley & Sons, 2019), pp. 349–71, p. 360.

136 Sinfield, 'Boys, Class and Gender', p. 166. In relation to the characterisation of Michael, Sinfield draws upon Harry Benshoff's use of the term 'inoculation' in reference to the treatment of homosexuality in horror films. See Harry M. Benshoff, *Monsters in the Closet* (Manchester: Manchester University Press, 1997), p. 188.

137 Sinfield, 'Boys, Class and Gender', p. 170.

138 Warbeck, interview with author.

139 Richardson, 'Gender, Sexuality and British Cinema', p. 358.

140 Weber, '"Oi, Dancing Boy!"'.

141 Barney Hoskyns, *Glam! Bowie, Bolan and the Glitter Rock Revolution* (London: Faber and Faber, 1998), p. 16.

142 The T. Rex song is not the last to appear on the soundtrack, however. The credits continue with 'I Believe' by Stephen Gately, a newly written ballad for the singer best known at the time as a member of the Irish boyband Boyzone, with aspirational lyrics that roughly connect with the film's premise ('Could I spread my wings and say goodbye', etc.). The song's inclusion brings the film into line with other Working Title soundtrack strategies (such as that of *Notting Hill*, which showcased Gately's Boyzone co-singer Ronan Keating), but Gately's coming out as gay in 1999, and his early death in 2009 from a congenital heart defect, add some metatextual poignancy. The final song on the credits is 'Burning Up' by Eagle-Eye Cherry, which featured on his *Living in the Present Future* album of 2000, and was likely chosen with the spin-off soundtrack album in mind, as its inclusion frustrates any meaningful analysis.

143 Christopher Tookey, 'I'm a veteran of over 7,000 films – but this British masterpiece beats them all', *Daily Mail* (26 September 2000), p. 11.

144 Gilbert Adair, 'One of those films destined to be forgotten', *Independent* (12 November 2000), Features, p. 1.

145 Nathan Townsend, *Working Title Films: A Creative and Commercial History* (Edinburgh: Edinburgh University Press, 2020), p. 208.
146 The 'Billy Idiot' sketch was part of the *Lenny Henry in Pieces* Christmas special, broadcast on 30 December 2000.
147 'Death of a Member: Baroness Thatcher', *Hansard* HL Deb. 744, 10 April 2013. Available at: <https://hansard.parliament.uk/Lords/2013-04-10/debates/1304101000196/DeathOfAMemberBaronessThatcher?highlight=%22billy%20elliot%22> (accessed 2 May 2024).
148 The song 'Merry Christmas, Maggie Thatcher', which opens the second half of the stage musical, features the following lyrics in its chorus refrain: 'Merry Christmas, Maggie Thatcher / We all celebrate today / 'Cause it's one day closer to your death'.
149 'Her Late Majesty Queen Elizabeth II', *Hansard* HL Deb. 824, 10 September 2022. Available at: <https://hansard.parliament.uk/Lords/2022-09-10/debates/1A292C36-9BBE-4B5A-9366-ADD0154812E5/HerLateMajestyQueenElizabethII?highlight=she%20obliged%20perform%20own%20role%20dress#contribution-9A008467-2B22-4690-814E-DC6C9B34FAAC> (accessed 2 May 2024).
150 Robert Pattinson, 'Jamie Bell', *Interview* (20 July 2015). Available at: <https://www.interviewmagazine.com/film/jamie-bell> (accessed 5 May 2024).
151 Forrest, *Kes*, p. 42.
152 Bell performed the Billy Casper role in a production of *Kes* at the ARC Stockton Arts Centre in March 2000.
153 Philip Kemp, '*Hallam Foe*', *Sight and Sound* 17, no. 9 (September 2007), p. 59.
154 Arjun Sajip, 'Q&A: Andrew Haigh', *Sight and Sound* 34, no. 1 (Winter 2023/4), p. 11.
155 Jane Kelly, 'As a star of the blockbuster film shuns the screen for the Army: how Billy Elliot ruined my life', *Daily Mail* (21 December 2001), p. 11.
156 Charles Gant, 'The Numbers: 2014 in Review', *Sight and Sound* 25, no. 2 (February 2015), p. 15.
157 Robert Gordon, '*Billy Elliot* and its Lineage: The Politics of Class and Sexual Identity in British Musicals Since 1953', in Robert Gordon and Olaf Jubin (eds), *The Oxford Handbook of the British Musical* (New York: Oxford University Press, 2017), pp. 419–44, p. 421.
158 Hall, interview with author.
159 Lee Hall, *The Pitmen Painters* (London: Faber and Faber, 2008), p. viii.
160 Hall, interview with author.
161 Peter Matthews, '*Sweet Sixteen*', *Sight and Sound* 12, no. 10 (October 2002), p. 56.
162 Louis Bayman, 'Can There be a Progressive Nostalgia? Layering Time in *Pride*'s Retro-Heritage', *Special Collection: Pride Revisited: Cinema, Activism and Re-Activation, Open Library of Humanities* 5, no. 1 (2019). Available at: <https://olh.openlibhums.org/article/id/4556/> (accessed 4 June 2024).
163 Elton John, *Me* (London: Pan Macmillan, 2019), p. 293.
164 See Leggott, *In Fading Light*, pp. 170–205.
165 Katy Shaw, *Mining the Meaning: Cultural Representations of the 1984–5 UK Miners' Strike* (Newcastle upon Tyne: Cambridge Scholars, 2012), p. 191.

166 Niall Richardson, '"What I was told about lesbians really did shock me. It can't be true, can it? You're all vegetarians?": Greywashing Gay Shame in *Pride*', *Special Collection: Pride Revisited: Cinema, Activism and Re-Activation*, *Open Library of Humanities* 6, no. 1 (2020). Available at: <https://olh.openlibhums.org/article/id/4611/> (accessed 2 June 2024).
167 Finn, interview with author.
168 Hall, interview with author.
169 Not forgetting that Loach had previously represented the people of the Durham coalfields in the period drama *Days of Hope* (1975) and the 1984 documentary *Which Side Are You On?* about the music and poetry of the miners' strike.
170 Alan Franks, 'Let's dance', *The Times* (13 October 2001), pp. 34–5, p. 34.
171 Catherine Milner, 'More boys than girls join the Royal Ballet', *Sunday Telegraph* (14 April 2002), p. 9.
172 Hannah Furness, 'Billy Elliot effect of getting working class boys into dance is a myth, says Royal Ballet star', *Telegraph* (27 October 2016), p. 36.
173 Louise Levene, 'Billy boys and bully boys', *Financial Times* (18 April 2020), p. 12.
174 David Sanderson, 'Billy effect leads to shortage of ballerinas', *The Times* (9 December 2015), p. 4.
175 Rob Parsons, 'The "Billy Elliot effect" still putting people in the North East off creative careers four decades on', *Evening Chronicle* (19 January 2022). Available at: <https://www.chroniclelive.co.uk/news/north-east-news/billy-elliot-effect-still-putting-22793107> (accessed 1 June 2024).
176 Nick James, 'A Matter of Tone', p. 5.

BILLY ELLIOT | 99

Credits

Billy Elliot
UK
2000

Directed by
Stephen Daldry
Produced by
Greg Brenman
Jon Finn
Screenplay
Lee Hall
Executive Producers
Natascha Wharton
Charles Brand
Tessa Ross
David M. Thompson
Choreographer
Peter Darling
Director of Photography
Brian Tufano
Editor
John Wilson
Production Designer
Maria Djurkovic
Costume Designer
Stewart Meacham
Composer
Stephen Warbeck
Casting
Jina Jay
Line Producer
Tori Parry
Hair and Make-up Designer
Ivana Primorac
Production Sound Mixer
Mark Holding Amps

© 2000 Tiger Aspect Pictures Ltd

Production Companies
Working Title Films and
BBC Films
in association with the
Arts Council of England
present
A Tiger Aspect Pictures
Production
in association with WT²

First Assistant Director
Martin Harrison
Production Accountant
Gary Nixon
Associate Choreographer
Lynne Page
Focus Puller
Robert Shipsey
Clapper Loaders
Clive Pittman
Ed Jones
Camera Grip
David Maund
Camera Trainees
Joanne Lee
Hayley Ann Farr
Script Supervisor
Zoe Morgan
Sound Maintenance
Richard Finney
Peter Eusebe
Sound Trainee
Michael Yallop
Production Co-ordinator
Francesca Dowd
Production Assistant
Deborah Willey
Second Assistant Director
Finn McGrath

Third Assistant Director
Mike Hanley
Floor Runner
Ann Cattrall
Additional Photography
Robert Shipsey
Second Unit Director of Photography
Robert Fabbri
First Assistant Director
Alison Banks
Second Assistant Director
Alexander Bignell
Third Assistant Director
Aurelia Thomas
Floor Runner
Nick Simmons
Executive in Charge of Production
Angela Morrison
WT² Company Co-ordinator
Amanda Boyle
Assistant to Stephen Daldry
Marieke Spencer
Assistant to Greg Brenman
Katie Waters
Assistant to Natascha Wharton
Rachel Prior
Script Editor
Roanna Benn
Producer Runner
Darren Price
Production Office Trainee
Dylan Southern

Assistant Accountant
Matthew O'Toole
First Assistant Editor
Mark Eckersley
Second Assistant Editors
Emily Grant
Will MacNeil
Supervising Sound Editor
Zane Hayward
Dialogue and ADR Editor
Stewart Henderson
Foley Editor
Anthony Faust
Music Supervisor
Nick Angel
Re-recording Mixer
Mike Prestwood Smith
Assistant Re-recording Mixer
Matthew Gough
ADR Recordists
Darren McQuade
Ted Swanscott
Foley Recordists
Hugh Johnson
Ted Swanscott
Hair/Make-up Artist
Nikita Rae
Costume Supervisor
Alison Goss
Costume Assistants
Melissa Layton
Carla Pope
Art Director
Adam O'Neill
Standby Art Director
Anthony Caron-Delion
Set Decorator
Tatiana Lund
Assistant Buyer
Ann Taylor
Art Department Assistant/Graphics
Stelios Polychronakis
Storyboard Artist
Stephen Forrest-Smith
Sign Writer
Goggi Lund
Prop Master
Alan Bailey
Storeman/Dresser
Nick Mollo
Chargehand/Standby
David Fisher
Standby Prop
Billy Edwards
Dressing Prop
Ron Higgins
Location Managers
Christine Llewellyn-Reeve
Joseph Jayawardena
Unit Manager Durham
Nick Waldron
Assistant Location Manager
David Medlycott
Location Finder
Sue Quinn
Location Runner
Ashley Horner
Casting Associates
Shaheen Baig
Pippa Hall
Chloe Emmerson
Additional Help
Paddy O'Connor
Kayin Cheng
Sarah Rule
For Tiger Aspect Business Affairs
Jenny Lalor
Tiger Aspect Development Executive
Amanda Davis
For Working Title
Rachel Holroyd
Working Title Business Affairs
Çigdem Worthington
Julian Tomlin
Financial Controller for the BBC
Julie Scott
BBC Production Executive
Grainne Marmion
Construction Manager
John Bohan
Supervising Carpenters
Robert Wishart
Thomas Martin
Supervising Painters
Paul Wescott
Clive Ward
Standby Carpenter
Cathal MacIlwaine
Standby Rigger
Edward Pearce
Standby Painter
Ian Williamson (Durham)
Gaffer Electrician
Liam McGill
Best Boy
Iwan Williams
Electricians
Gary Nolan
Martin Welland
Generator Operator
Brian McGivern

SFX Supervisor
Stuart Murdoch
SFX Technician
Daniel Wright
Dialect Coach
Jill McCullough
Tutors
Ann Hetherington
Katherine Hook
Chaperones for Jamie Bell
Eileen Bell
Audrey Matfin
Unit Publicist
Nevette Previd, Freud Communications
Stills Photographer
Giles Keyte
Health and Safety Advisors
Cyril Gibbons
Jake Edmonds
Unit Nurses
Cath Nevin
Cate Brockbank
Stand-ins
Elsie Koerner
Michael Whitcomb
Rachel Burgess
Stunt Co-ordinator
Lee Sheward
Stunt Performers
Richard Bradshaw
Neil Finnighan
Steve Street Griffin
Richard Hammatt
Paul Heasman
Nick Hobbs
Rob Inch
Andrew Lambert
Derek Lea
Ray L. Nicholas
Seon Rogers
C.C. Smiff
Mark Southworth
Alan Stuart
Visual Effects
Double Negative
Opticals and Titles
Cine Image
Post-production Consultancy
Steeple Post Production Services
Post-production Co-ordinator
Emma Zee
Post-production Accountant
Tarn Harper
Unit Drivers
Sonny Donato
Tony Russell
Jeff Oldman
Terry Reece
David Walls
Stewart Thompson
Brett Curran
Camera Truck Driver
Dale Wilson
Wardrobe Truck/ Make-up Truck
Daniel Brown
Dining Bus Driver
Paul Brosnan
Standby Construction Driver
John Cornelius
Standby Props Driver
Vick Todd
Prop Runaround Driver
Keith West
Construction Driver
Barry Gibbs
Action Vehicles
Action Vehicles
Catering Supplied by
GT Caterers
Wood Hall Catering
Head Chefs
Sean Gobbi
Andy Bailey
Caterers
Mick Norfolk
John Wood
Gus Williamson
Matt Harvey
Editing Equipment
Hyperactive Broadcast
Sound Editing Equipment
Atlantic Post Production
Electric Equipment
Lee Lighting
Aaton Camera Supplied by
I. C. E. Films
Negative Cutting
Professional Negative Cutting
Laboratory
Technicolor Film Services
Laboratory Contact
John Ensby
Colour Grader
Peter Ferrari
ADR Recording Studios
Mag Masters
Videosonics
De Lane Lea

Post-production Facilities
De Lane Lea
Stills Processing
Pinewood Stills
Transport/Facilities Supplied by
On Set Location Services
Rushes Courier Services
A. E. I. UK
Horses Supplied by
Timber Tops
Costumiers
Angels and Bermans
Studio 4 Costumes
BBC Costumes
Ray Marston Wig Studio
Insurance Services Supplied by
Aon/Albert G. Ruben
Legal Services Supplied by
Marriott Harrison
Completion Bond
Film Finances, Inc.
Post-production Script by
Sapex Scripts

The appearance of Mr Fred Astaire has been arranged through a special licence with Mrs Fred Astaire, Beverly Hills, California. All rights reserved.

The *Top Hat* clip appears courtesy Turner Entertainment Co.

'Top Hat, White Tie and Tails', performed by Fred Astaire, courtesy of Turner Entertainment Co., composed by Irving Berlin, Irving Berlin Music Corp. By kind permission of Warner/Chappell Music Limited

Swan Lake appears courtesy of Adventures in Motion Pictures Limited and Matthew Bourne

Orchestration
Stephen Warbeck
Conductor
Nick Ingman
Composer's Assistant
Andrew Green
Orchestral Contractor
Isobel Griffiths
Piano
Dave Hartley
Orchestra Leader
Rolf Wilson
Cello Solo
Anthony Pleeth
Guitars
John Parricelli
Bass
Andy Pask
Drums
Ian Thomas
Violin
Mark Berrow
Cello
Paul Kegg

Viola
Bruce White
Music Copying and Preparations
Graham Read
Music Recorded and Mixed by
Chris Dibble, C. T. S. Studio
Lansdowne Recording Studios
Special Thanks to
Archibalds Builders Merchants; Arts, Libraries & Museums Department, Durham County Council; Lisa Bailey; Joanie Blaikie; Brehon & Co. Solicitors; British Coal Corporation; Byrons Casting; The Coal Authority; Coastal Productions; Durham Constabulary; Easington District Council; Gretta Finer; Gerry Gore; Krackers Kids; Middlesborough Council; Newcastle upon Tyne Council; Northern Screen Commission; Northfield School; Northumbria Police; Kevin O'Shea; Paris Helen School of Dance; Janet Plater; Patsy Pollock; Seaham Town Council; Stagecoach Theatre Arts Schools Salisbury; Nicole Uprichard; West London

School of Dance; Thomas A. White; David Wilder; Graham Wynn

Soundtrack
'A Child is Born', written by Thad Jones, performed and arranged by Douglas Corbin, courtesy of Bodarc Productions, Dallas, TX, USA; 'Children of the Revolution', words and music by Marc Bolan, performed by T. Rex, issued under licence from Crimson Productions, a division of the Demon Music Group Ltd; 'Cosmic Dancer', words and music by Marc Bolan, performed by T. Rex, courtesy of Straight Ahead Productions Limited; 'Get It On', words and music by Marc Bolan, performed by T. Rex, courtesy of Straight Ahead Productions Limited; 'I Love to Boogie', words and music by Marc Bolan, performed by T. Rex, issued under licence from Crimson Productions, a division of the Demon Music Group Ltd; 'I Believe', written by Steve Mac/Wayne Hector, performed by Stephen Gately, courtesy of Polydor UK Limited; 'London Calling', written by Joe Strummer/Mick Jones/Paul Simonon/Topper Headon, courtesy of Columbia Records/Sony Music Entertainment (UK) Ltd; 'Ride a White Swan', words and music by Marc Bolan, performed by T. Rex, courtesy of Straight Ahead Productions Limited; 'Town Called Malice', written and composed by Paul Weller, performed by The Jam, courtesy of Polydor UK Limited; 'Burning Up', written by Eagle-Eye Cherry, performed by Eagle-Eye Cherry, courtesy of Polydor UK Limited

Soundtrack album available on Polydor

Developed by
BBC Films
Supported by
The National Lottery through the Arts Council of England
Camera and Lenses by
Arri Media

Originated on Motion Picture Film Supplied by
Kodak Motion Picture Imaging
Dedicated to
Ian Ritchie
Ted Rogers

CAST
Jamie Bell
Billy
Jean Heywood
Grandma
Jamie Draven
Tony
Gary Lewis
Dad
Stuart Wells
Michael
Mike Elliot
George Watson
Billy Fane
Mr Braithwaite
Nicola Blackwell
Debbie
Julie Walters
Mrs Wilkinson
Carol McGuigan
librarian
Joe Renton
Gary Poulson
Colin MacLachlan
Mr Wilkinson
Janine Birkett
Billy's mum
Trevor Fox
PC Jeff Peverly
Charlie Hardwick
Sheila Briggs

Danny Ferguson
miner
Dennis Lingard
NCB official
Matthew Thomas
Simon
Stephen Mangan
ballet doctor
Paul Ridley
tutor in medical
Patrick Malahide
Principal
Barbara Leigh-Hunt
Vice-Principal
Imogen Claire
tutor 1
Diana Kent
tutor 2

Neil North
tutor 3
Lee Williams
tutor 4
Petra Siniawksi
teacher
Merelina Kendall
secretary
Zoe Bell
Sandra
Tracey Wilkinson
Geography teacher
Merryn Owen
Michael (aged 25)
Adam Cooper
Billy (aged 25)

Production Details
Made on location
in County Durham
and London and at
Shepperton Studios,
London, England.
35mm
1.85:1
Colour
Dolby Digital
MPAA no.: 37443
Running time:
110 minutes

Release Details
UK theatrical release
on 29 September 2000
by United International
Pictures
US theatrical release
on 13 October 2000 by
Universal Focus